Historic Kirkcaldy

the archaeological implications of development

E P Dennison **Torrie**

Russel **Coleman**

the Scottish burgh survey

HISTORIC SCOTLAND

in association with

SCOTTISH CULTURAL PRESS

CENTRE FOR SCOTTISH URBAN HISTORY
Department of Scottish History
University of Edinburgh

FIFE

publication	Historic Scotland *in association with* Scottish Cultural Press First published 1995
copyright	© Historic Scotland 1995 *The moral right of the authors has been asserted.*
editorial	Olwyn Owen
design	Christina Unwin
printing . binding	British Printing Company, Aberdeen
ISSN	1358 0272
Scottish Cultural Press ISBN	1 898218 38 2
all distribution and sales enquiries	Scottish Cultural Press PO Box 106 Aberdeen AB9 8ZE telephone *01224* 583777 . facsimile *01224* 575337
all other enquiries	■ Scottish burgh surveys Centre for Scottish Urban History Department of Scottish History University of Edinburgh EH8 9LN telephone *0131* 650 4032 . facsimile *0131* 650 4032 ■ Historic Scotland Longmore House Salisbury Place Edinburgh EH9 1SH telephone *0131* 668 8600 . facsimile *0131* 668 8699
British Library cataloguing in publication data	A catalogue record for this book is available from the British Library

contents

preface   This account of the history and archaeology of Kirkcaldy is one of a series of reports on the historic burghs of Scotland—known collectively as the *Scottish Burgh Survey*—all of which have been commissioned by **Historic Scotland** and its predecessors. Some 56 burghs have been surveyed during previous campaigns of the Scottish Burgh Survey (1978–90), but *Historic Kirkcaldy* marks an important milestone for this is the first time that a burgh survey has been formally published. It is hoped that most, if not all, future burgh surveys will be published and that, in time, some of the existing burgh surveys may be updated and published too.

The main aim of *Historic Kirkcaldy* is to identify those areas in the historic burgh which are of archaeological interest and therefore require sensitive treatment in the event of any proposed development or other ground disturbance. It is designed primarily as a working manual for the use of local authorities and archaeological curators. However, as an essential prerequisite to this assessment of the archaeological implications of development, it also describes and illustrates the geography and geology of the town, its known archaeology and history, its historic standing buildings and the origins of its street names—all of which will be of interest to the wider public, be they inhabitant, visitor or student.

Historic Kirkcaldy was prepared for Historic Scotland within the **Centre for Scottish Urban History**, which is part of the Department of Scottish History, University of Edinburgh. Dr E P Dennison Torrie, Director of the Centre for Scottish Urban History, and Russel Coleman, of the **Scottish Urban Archaeological Trust**, are co-authors of the report. Kevin Hicks, of the **Centre for Field Archaeology**, University of Edinburgh, is cartographer and illustrator, and Alan MacDonald of the Department of Scottish History acted as research assistant. The project is supervised by the Head of the Department, Professor Michael Lynch, and managed for Historic Scotland by Olwyn Owen, Inspector of Ancient Monuments.

In this first published survey, Historic Scotland acknowledges with gratitude the help of the **Scottish Burgh Survey Working Group** whose advice on the selection of burghs for survey in 1994, and on a new format for the surveys (seen for the first time in *Historic Kirkcaldy*), has been invaluable: John Gerrard (Scottish Civic Trust), Professor Michael Lynch (Department of Scottish History, University of Edinburgh), Geoffrey Stell (Royal Commission on the Ancient and Historical Monuments of Scotland) and Dr Carol Swanson (Regional Archaeologist, Strathclyde Regional Council). Lorna Main (Regional Archaeologist, Central Region) and Judith Stones (Archaeologist, Aberdeen District Council) also provided valuable advice during the formative stages of the present project. The Scottish Burgh Survey owes a particular debt to Geoffrey Stell who, having contributed so much to the project over many years, has also been involved during preparations for its re-commencement this year.

This survey of historic Kirkcaldy was entirely funded by Historic Scotland. The report has been published with financial assistance from **Kirkcaldy District Council**, **Fife Regional Council** and Historic Scotland. Further copies may be obtained from **Scottish Cultural Press**, PO Box 106, Aberdeen AB9 8ZE.

cover notes

The Kirkcaldy Penny A copper trade token of 1797. Although normally valued at one penny, this extremely fine token was probably produced as a private piece, struck for the designer R Boog Junior as a gift to friends or for exchange with other collectors. The dies were sunk by Wyon in London and it was manufactured by Kempson of Birmingham. The obverse is shown on the left, the reverse on the right.

As no significant copper coins were issued between the Union and the 1790s, the resultant dearth of small change was a great hardship to the ordinary people. This led to the striking of local token coinage in many places in the 1780s and 1790s. These 'trade tokens' were produced by shops and businesses and could be exchanged for goods at local shops. They fell out of use as currency after the large official issue of copper coins of George III in 1806–7.

The Centre for Scottish Urban History is indebted to a number of people for their
assistance and advice.

Especial thanks go to **Fife Regional Council** and **Kirkcaldy District Council**, in particular to Mr Peter Yeoman, Fife Archaeological Service, Department of Economy and Planning, Fife Region, and his assistant, Ms Sarah Govan; the Director of Engineering, Fife Region and the Roads Department, in particular Ralph Dean and John Wharne; Ms Dallas Mechan, Curator of Kirkcaldy District Museums, and her staff; Ms Janet Klakk, Reference Librarian, Kirkcaldy District Libraries; the Director of Planning, Kirkcaldy District Council, and in particular Mr Morton; and Ms Moira Wilson of Central Services, Town House Kirkcaldy.

Mr Robert Scrimgeour, chartered architect, and Mr Ted Ruddock of the **Scottish Historic Buildings Trust** gave us a most informative visit to 339–343 High Street, and an insight into their extensive researches on the property and its setting. We have benefited also from discussions with Professor Charles McKean, formerly Secretary to the **Royal Incorporation of Architects in Scotland**.

The **Scottish Urban Archaeological Trust** has been supportive, and the assistance of David Bowler, Derek Hall and Roy Cachart has been particularly appreciated. Dr Colin Martin of the Scottish History Department, **University of St Andrews**, has advised us on the maritime archaeological potential of the burgh.

Colleagues at the **University of Edinburgh** have given invaluable support and advice. In particular we would like to mention the Centre of Field Archaeology, Professor R J Morris of the Department of Economic and Social History, Dr Ian Morrison of the Department of Geography and Mr Simon Taylor of the School for Scottish Studies.

The **Royal Commission on the Ancient and Historical Monuments of Scotland** has been particularly supportive. The following should especially be mentioned: Dr Iain Fraser, Ms Diana Murray, Ms Rebecca Maloney, Dr Gordon Maxwell and Mr Geoffrey Stell.

The staff of the **Scottish Record Office** and of the **National Library of Scotland**, at both George IV Bridge and at the Map Library at Causewayside, have been extremely helpful. Mr George Dalgleish of the **National Museums of Scotland** kindly provided information about the Kirkcaldy Penny.

To all of these we extend our thanks.

cover *The Kirkcaldy Penny* is reproduced by kind permission of the **Trustees of the National Museums of Scotland**. © *Crown Copyright: NMS.*

figure 2 is reproduced by kind permission of the Ministry of Defence. © *Crown Copyright: MOD.*

figure 4 is reproduced by kind permission of **Fife Regional Council**.

figures 5 & **19** are reproduced by kind permission of the **Trustees of the National Library of Scotland**.

figures 6, 7, 14 & **16** are reproduced by kind permission of **Kirkcaldy Museum and Art Gallery**. We are grateful to Kirkcaldy Museums for their kind contribution.

figures 8–12, 15, 17 & **18** are based upon the 1989 Ordnance Survey 1:10,000 scale and the 1965–82 Ordnance Survey 1:2,500 map series, with permission of **The Controller of Her Majesty's Stationery Office**. © *Crown Copyright.*

figure 13 is reproduced by kind permission of the **Royal Commission on Ancient and Historical Monuments of Scotland**. © *Crown Copyright: RCAHMS.*

abbreviations

APS	*The Acts of the Parliaments of Scotland*, 12 vols, edd T Thomson & C Innes (Edinburgh, 1814–75).
CDS	J Bain (ed), *Calendar of Documents relating to Scotland*, 4 vols (Edinburgh, 1881–8).
DES	*Discovery and Excavation in Scotland.*
Dunf Recs	*The Burgh Records of Dunfermline*, ed E Beveridge (Edinburgh, 1917).
Dunf Reg	*Registrum de Dunfermlyn*, ed C Innes (Bannatyne Club, 1842).
ER	*The Exchequer Rolls of Scotland*, 23 vols, edd J Stuart *et al* (Edinburgh, 1878–1908).
KBR	*The Kirkcaldy Burgh Records*, ed L MacBean (Kirkcaldy, 1908).
NSA	*The New Statistical Account of Scotland* (Edinburgh, 1845).
OSA	*The Old Statistical Account of Scotland*, 1791–1799, ed Sir John Sinclair. New edition, edd D J Withrington & I R Grant (Wakefield, 1973).
PPS	*Proceedings of the Prehistoric Society.*
PSAS	*Proceedings of the Society of Antiquaries of Scotland.*
RCRB	*The Records of the Convention of Royal Burghs of Scotland*, 7 vols, ed J D Marwick (Edinburgh 1866–1918).
RMS	*The Register of the Great Seal of Scotland*, 11 vols, edd J M Thomson *et al* (Edinburgh, 1882–1914).
RPC	*The Register of the Privy Council of Scotland*, edd J H Burton *et al* (Edinburgh, 1877–).
RSS	*Register of the Privy Seal of Scotland (Registrum Secreti Sigilli Regum Scotorum)*, edd M Livingstone *et al* (Edinburgh, 1908–).
SHS	Scottish History Society.
SRO	Scottish Record Office, Edinburgh.
SUAT	Scottish Urban Archaeological Trust.
TA	*Accounts of the (Lord High) Treasurer of Scotland*, edd T Dickson *et al* (Edinburgh, 1877–).

summary

1   Use the colour-coded map on p 58 **figure 18** and/or the **general index** to locate a particular site (normally the site of a development proposal).

2   If the site is in a **blue area**, any development proposal is unlikely to affect significant archaeological remains. No action needed.

3   If the site is in a **green area**, it is possible that any proposal involving ground disturbance may encounter archaeological remains. Green areas are designated as having archaeological potential. Seek appropriate archaeological advice as early as possible.

4   Use the map on p 26 **figure 8** to determine which area of the burgh the site falls into (one of Areas 1–6), and turn to the relevant area in **area by area assessment**.

5   Use the **general index** and, if appropriate, the index of **street names** for rapid access to information specific to a site, street or named feature of the town.

step 1

As a working manual, the first point of reference is the colour-coded map on p 58 **figure 18**.

The **green areas** are **archaeologically sensitive** areas and may retain significant subsurface archaeological information. Consultation should take place with the Regional Archaeologist, where *any development proposal or enquiry involving ground disturbance* is being considered, including car parks, road schemes, environmental improvements, landscaping and drainage schemes, as well as the usual range of development and redevelopment proposals in built-up areas. There is no necessity for a consultation where ground disturbance is not in prospect, such as applications for change of use of a building. If in doubt whether consultation is necessary, please refer to the Regional Archaeologist. It is important to note that sub-surface disturbance within standing buildings may also affect archaeological remains, and that some standing buildings may retain archaeological features within their structures. Please seek advice as required.

Blue areas denote those parts of the historic burgh which may be **archaeologically sterile** and where archaeological consultation is probably not necessary. In practice, *there is rarely a hard dividing line between the green and the blue areas.*

step 2

In this new series of burgh surveys, each survey has been organised locationally, in order to assist speedy consultation on any proposed development site. In the case of Kirkcaldy, the historic core of the town has been divided into six arbitrary areas, Areas 1–6, which are shown on the plan on p 26 **figure 8**. The second step for the user then is to consult this plan and determine into which area a specific enquiry falls.

It should be noted here that Kirkcaldy lies on an approximate north-west to south-east axis. Early documentary sources at times invite confusion by treating the town as if it lay on an east–west axis, hence 'East Port' and 'West Port'. In this assessment East Port is to the north of the town, West Port to the south and the sea to the east.

step 3

In **area by area assessment**, each area is considered individually, the commentary prefaced with a detailed plan of that area. Archaeological, historical, geographical and geological

2

factors of particular relevance to the area are all discussed, and an assessment of the archaeological potential is made. For ease of reference, even if a dividing line between areas is shown as the middle of a street, discussion of the area includes any elements within the street up to the opposite frontage. The importance of an integrated approach to the historical and archaeological information is implicit in the design of this report: the history and archaeology are presented together on each page rather than consecutively.

This integrated, area-based approach has involved some repetition of information in the area by area assessment, in order that users are not required to cross-reference more than necessary when dealing with a specific enquiry. For instance, the siting, nature and use of the town ports is discussed in all those areas where a port is located, or may have been situated. Although such repetition would not be normal in a work of interest to the general public, it was felt that it would be permissible here in order to facilitate the work of primary users: local authority planners and other curators of the archaeological resource.

historic standing buildings

historic buildings reinforces the above sections by providing basic historical information about the historic standing buildings of the town and, where relevant, their area location and an assessment of their archaeological potential. It should always be borne in mind that historic standing buildings may also contain archaeological remains, both beneath their floors and within their structures, as amply testified in Kirkcaldy at 339–343 High Street (p 61).

objectives for future fieldwork and research

Any report of this nature cannot be definitive. During its preparation, a series of archaeological and historical objectives for future fieldwork and research have been identified; these are listed at pp 67–9. They will be of particular interest to urban historians and archaeologists, and to those responsible for management of the archaeological resource in historic Kirkcaldy.

referencing

The report contains a comprehensive **general index** as well as a listing of **street names** giving basic historical information and, where relevant, the area of location.

All archive reports of small-scale archaeological work are housed in the **National Monuments Record** John Sinclair House, 16 Bernard Terrace, Edinburgh, EH8 9NX, telephone *0131* 662 1456, facsimile *0131* 662 1477/1499.

full reference to this report Torrie, E P Dennison & Coleman, R 1995 *Historic Kirkcaldy: the archaeological implications of development*, published by Historic Scotland in association with Scottish Cultural Press, Aberdeen. (Scottish Burgh Survey 1995).

the Scottish burgh survey

4

Kirkcaldy

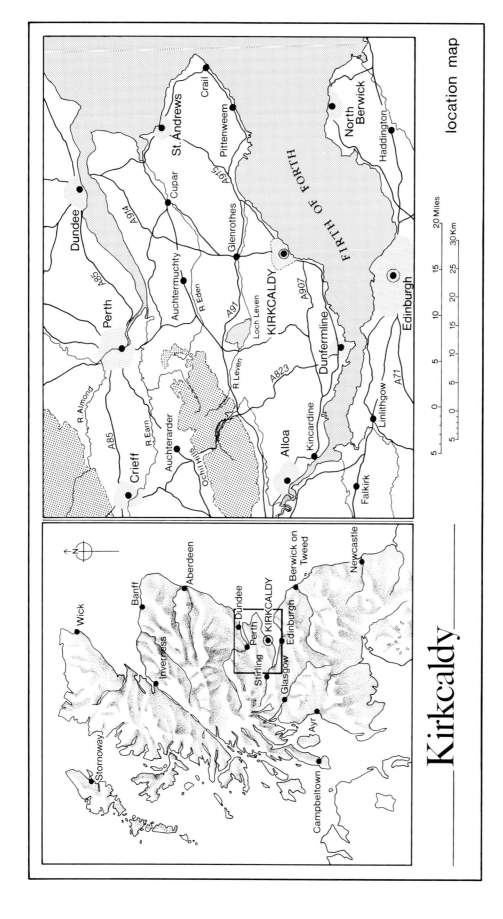

location map

figure 1

Location of Kirkcaldy

geographical location

Kirkcaldy is situated on the south-east coast of Fife, in the busy sea-lane of the Firth of Forth, and between the coastal burghs of Kinghorn and Dysart **figure 1**. Kirkcaldy was close to two of the most important ecclesiastical and secular centres in Scotland, St Andrews and Dunfermline, and on or near two main route-ways—connecting Edinburgh and the south with the north (Perth), and with the north-east (Dundee, Arbroath, Aberdeen and into Moray). Fifteen of the eighteen royal burghs in Fife were coastal ports, emphasising the strategic and commercial importance of these harbour towns on the North Sea network, and reflecting the important trading links that these towns had with France, the Low Countries and the Baltic.

geology

Tectonic movements along two major dislocations of the earth's crust, the Southern Uplands Fault and the Highland Boundary Fault, have created three principal structural and physiographic divisions—the Highlands, the Midland Valley and the Southern Uplands.[1]

Kirkcaldy lies in the Midland Valley of Scotland, the name given to the relatively low lying central part of Scotland situated between the Grampian Highlands and the Southern Uplands. However, physiographically the area is more diverse than the name suggests. Much of the region consists of farmland lying below 180 m, but there are many upland areas of rough pasture and moorland.

The landscape around Kirkcaldy is primarily a product of the postglacial period (Holocene), characterised by a series of raised beaches. In the north of Britain, and elsewhere, the loss of the great weight of the ice sheets caused the land to rise, a phenomenon known as 'isostatic uplift'. As the water, locked up for so long, was released, worldwide ocean levels also began to rise. There then followed a complex interplay between the local rising of land, which varied from place to place in Scotland, and the rising world ocean level, as the ice sheets melted elsewhere after those of Scotland had melted. Peat beds, for example, of early postglacial age lie buried beneath marine clays in various places in the Firth of Forth, both upstream to the west and downstream to the east of Kirkcaldy. Later, as the ocean level rose faster than the local land, beach gravels were laid down, sometimes resting on an ancient rock-cut platform of lateglacial or interglacial age. Finally, the land emerged; many of these beaches, such as those at Kirkcaldy, now lie well above the reach of the sea.[2]

During the 1960s and 1970s a reappraisal of raised beaches took place: in particular of the so-called '25 foot' raised beach at Kirkcaldy, which represents one of the most significant landform changes to occur between 10,000 and 5,000 bp[3] in Scotland. This has laid the foundations for a series of research projects.[4]

The raised beach landscape at Kirkcaldy is important to this survey in that it almost certainly influenced the layout of the medieval burgh and its subsequent development. A more detailed study of this relationship, incorporating the research carried out by Smith for example, could be an avenue for further work well worth exploring.[5]

soils and agriculture

The parent materials of the soils around Kirkcaldy comprise raised beach sands and gravels derived from Carboniferous limestones and sandstones with some Old Red Sandstone material. Brown forest soils with some gleying characterise the component soils.[6]

The agricultural land around Kirkcaldy and in its hinterland is capable of producing a wide range of crops. Consistently high yields of a few crops (principally cereals and grass) are obtained, and moderate yields of a wide range of others (including potatoes, field-beans and other vegetables and root crops). The limitations are moderate, but include wetness and slightly unfavourable soil structure and texture.[7]

figure 2
Kirkcaldy from the air
© *Crown Copyright:*
MOD

topography and the physical setting of the burgh

The burgh itself lies at the base of several natural terraces which, in places, slope sharply eastwards down to the sea. To the north and south lie the East Burn and the Tiel Burn respectively, which empty into the sea, forming a long, natural sandy cove, alongside which the burgh developed **figure 2**.

The curving medieval High Street is curious in its alignment. However, when compared with a contour map of the local area produced for this survey, there appears to

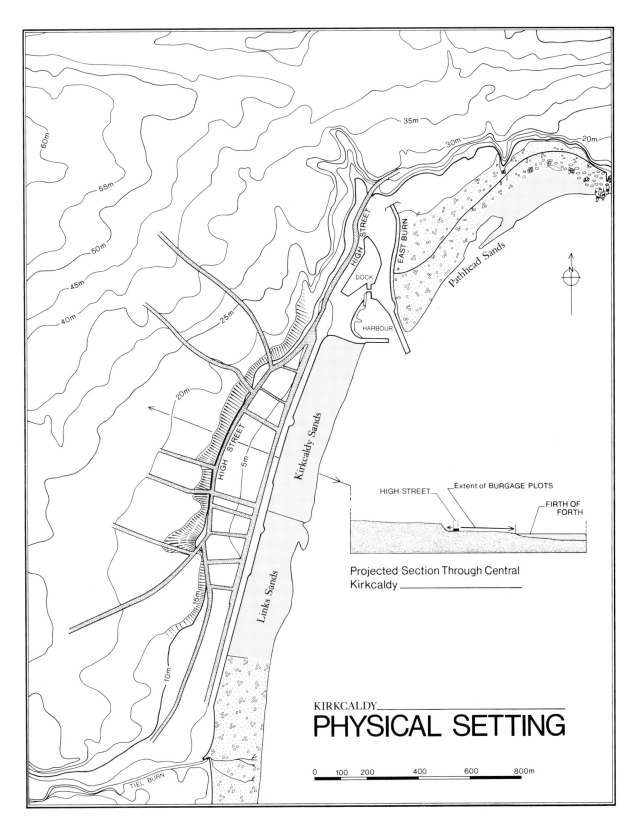

KIRKCALDY
PHYSICAL SETTING

0   100   200   400   600   800m

figure 3

The physical setting
of Kirkcaldy

be a direct relationship between the alignment of the High Street and the local topography. This suggests that the burgh developed, or was laid out deliberately, along the edge of a natural ridge, perhaps as near to the sea front as was physically possible **figure 3**. Although these are modern levels, an examination of the spot heights (Ordnance Datum) from the OS 1:10,000 map appears to confirm the presence of this ridge, which forms the 10 m contour line. It is one of a series of postglacial raised beaches that extend westwards from the sea.

The relationship identified here, between local topography and the morphology of the medieval burgh, is important for this study. Firstly, it highlights the impact of the physical

8

environment on first settlement, and the constraints it imposed on the subsequent development of the burgh; secondly, it may help to pinpoint the original nucleus of the early settlement.

In general, the ground level along the High Street is fairly constant, but there is a slight rise at the junction of Whytescauseway (*c* 11 m OD). The streets and wynds that extend eastwards from the High Street continue down from this ridge, a fall of at least 5 m, to the lowest of the terraces which marks the Mean High Water Spring Tides. Much of this area was raised in the 1920s to form the Esplanade.

To the west of the High Street, the narrow wynds and streets climb steeply up the slope to the next ridge, situated at a height of *c* 15 m OD. The rise in the ground level here is significant and, for this reason, there appears to have been artificial terracing to reduce the impact of the slope. The extent of the slope here may also have been a limiting factor in the westward development of the burgh, resulting in a narrow strip of settlement along the west side of the High Street. In contrast, the plots on the east side may originally have been much longer, extending further down a more gradual slope to the sea shore (*see* **figure 3**). A cartographic study of the Moore and Wood maps, of 1809 and 1824 respectively, appears to confirm this interpretation (*see* **figure 19**).

Southwards from the West Port, the ridge on which the High Street lies continues at around the same level (*c* 9 m OD), gently curving towards Linktown. Northwards beyond the East Port (Port Brae), towards the end of the High Street/Sailors' Walk, the ground falls away to *c* 5 m OD before climbing steeply to Pathhead and Ravenscraig Castle (*c* 31 m OD).

notes

1   Definitions according to J B Sissons, *The Geomorphology of the British Isles: Scotland* (London, 1976).
2   J V S Megaw & D D A Simpson, *Introduction to British Prehistory* (Leicester, 1979), 10
3   bp 'before present', 1950.
4   R J Price, *Scotland's Environment During the Last 30,000 Years* (Edinburgh, 1983), 154.
5   D E Smith, 'Late and Post Glacial Changes of Shoreline on the Northern Side of the Forth Valley and Estuary' (Unpublished University of Edinburgh PhD thesis, 1965).
6   C J Brown & B M Shipley, *Soil Survey of Scotland: South-East Scotland, 1:2,500,000 Sheet 7. Soil and Land Capability for Agriculture*, The Macaulay Institute for Soil Research (Aberdeen, 1982).
7   Brown & Shipley, *Soil Survey*.

archaeological and historical background

With relatively little archaeological work as yet undertaken in Kirkcaldy, and with at least as many prehistoric and Roman finds as medieval, the archaeological potential may be as high for the prehistoric period as the medieval. Therefore, a basic introduction to the prehistory and Roman history of the area has been included, in order to place archaeological finds in some sort of context, and to provide a broader framework within which to study the origins of the medieval burgh. A list of all previous work and chance finds, from in and around the burgh, follows this archaeological and historical background section.

prehistory

After the end of the Ice Age, some 9,000 years ago, Scotland was covered in dense woodland, which supported a rich variety of game, particularly red deer. It was to these herds that the earliest inhabitants of the Fife area owed their subsistence, following them through the seasons, while supplementing their diet with fish, wild plants and berries. This semi-nomadic existence has left little trace in the archaeological record. However at Morton, on the edge of Tentsmuir in north-east Fife (NO 467 227), a series of temporary camps has been discovered on what was, between 7,000 and 6,000 BC, an island, linked to the mainland only at low tide.

Changes in the environment, including more favourable soil conditions, together with ideas introduced from continental Europe around 3,500 BC, allowed the transition from a hunter-gatherer society to a more settled existence, brought about by farming. Chance finds from Kirkcaldy include four polished stone axes and a perforated axe and macehead. Although some of these may have been prestige goods, of social value to the owner, others may have been more utilitarian, used in the clearance of land for agriculture. Again, few traces of these settlements survive but the landscape of Fife still bears testament to their presence in the form of henges, stone circles and cist burials.

A henge, a circular space or platform, defined by an inner ditch and surrounded by an outer earthen bank within which timber posts, or occasionally, standing stones were erected, may have been the meeting place of these newly settled farming communities and the venue for a variety of rituals and ceremonies. An example of such a monument can be found at Balfarg, Glenrothes (NO 281 031), which was in use from around 3,000 BC for a period of nearly 1,500 years.

Stone circles, of which only one still survives in Fife, at Balbirnie (NT 285 029) near Glenrothes, though representing a different architectural tradition, perhaps performed similar functions for the community. Excavations at both Balfarg and Balbirnie have shown that, despite being built in the Neolithic period, these monuments were reused in the Bronze Age as burial grounds. This secondary use highlights the importance attached to these sites in the minds of subsequent generations.

Cist burials, of which eleven have been found from five separate sites within Kirkcaldy alone, represent the earliest known funerary tradition in the region, and date from between 2,500 BC and 500 BC. These consist of small, stone-lined graves containing a single body, laid on its side with the knees drawn up to the chest. Objects were often placed in the grave, perhaps for use in the afterlife, by relatives or those taking part in the funeral ceremony. The Kirkcaldy graves show a great deal of variety within this burial tradition, with some producing no grave goods or objects, although one was laid on a bed of rounded pebbles, while others produced pottery vessels known as Beakers, knives of flint and bronze, jet beads and buttons **figure 4**.

The number of cists found in Kirkcaldy is surprising and perhaps reflects the use of this area as a funerary landscape during this period. With the East Burn to the north and the Tiel Burn to the south, and with a series of natural terraces extending back from the curving sandy bay, this must have made an attractive setting, and perhaps provided a focal point in the landscape for the community.

Another common feature in the Bronze Age landscape of Fife was standing stones, examples of which can be seen at Lundin Links (NO 404 027) and Easter Pitcorthie (NO

10

figure 4
Bronze Age cist
burial.

497 039), near Colinsburgh. These can occur in groups or as single stones, and their function is unclear. They may define land boundaries, or, with burials and cremations occasionally present around them, as at Easter Pitcorthie, they may be burial memorials.

Cup and ring-marks, or shallow depressions, an art form dating from around 3,000 BC, are often to be seen carved into the faces of these standing stones, as well as on cist slabs and natural boulders. An example of a cup and ring-marked stone has been found built into the boundary wall of the old Raith Estate on the outskirts of Kirkcaldy (NT 261 914), though its place of origin remains unknown.

The end of the Bronze Age, around 600 BC, reflects considerable changes, not only in technology but also in society. Iron tools, and increasingly weapons as well, begin to appear in the archaeological record. In contrast to the abundance of evidence for monuments and rich burials in the Neolithic and Bronze Age, knowledge of the subsistence base which supported these societies and the settlements in which they lived is poor.[1] By the late Bronze Age/early Iron Age, the position is reversed and settlements begin to dominate the archaeological landscape. Numerous fortified settlements, ranging from large hillforts to enclosed villages and isolated single family dwellings, appear. Although other, less defensive types of settlements also existed, this emphasis on defence is generally seen as reflecting a more competitive society, perhaps fighting over natural resources, and a movement away from large monuments that served the community to more tribal divisions.

the Roman period

It was this more fragmented society that the Romans encountered in the first century AD. Ptolemy's map of Britain, dateable to around the same period, shows Fife as being the tribal territory of the Venicones. Little evidence of the Roman occupation of Scotland, however, can be seen in Fife. Only three temporary camps, which mark the route of military campaigns, have been identified: Bonnytown (NO 546 127), Auchtermuchty (NO 242 118) and Edenwood (NO 357 116). All three are thought to date to the final campaign in Scotland, led by Severus between AD 208 and AD 211. There is also a tradition of a Roman camp at Carberry Farm, on the outskirts of Kirkcaldy (NT 284 947), though nothing upstanding remains. For most of the four centuries of Roman occupation in

Britain, Hadrian's Wall formed the northern boundary of the Empire. The establishment of the Antonine Wall as the new northern frontier in the mid second century AD marked one of the many short-lived periods of advancement beyond Hadrian's Wall.

The Roman finds from Kirkcaldy, nine coins, all from separate find spots, represent an interesting assemblage, given the small number of Roman finds known in total from Fife and the relative absence of Roman sites. As yet, there are no real explanations for this cluster. The coins of the Severan period are probably attributable to increased military activity in eastern Scotland around this time, but may also represent the payment of subsidies to the local tribes.[2] Another explanation may be the presence, as yet undetected, of a port or camp, however temporary, in the area.

New research on the early Roman occupation of Scotland may lead to a reassessment of military strategy during the first century AD, and throw new light on native Fife at this time. There is evidence to suggest that Agricola, the Governor of Britain, rejected the Forth-Clyde isthmus as the northernmost limit of Roman rule in Britain, in favour of the River Tay.[3] Recent field and aerial photographic surveys have identified significant numbers of native settlement sites, in particular unenclosed hut circles, in northern and eastern Fife. These sites may be relevant to an assessment of Roman strategy, both in this and later periods of occupation. If there was a chain of forts along the Tay frontier from which to launch further campaigns, then the road between the Forth and the Tay would have been crucial in providing access to the frontier[4] **figure 5**. In order to protect this important line of communication, payments or subsidies were probably made to the local tribes, which might help to explain the concentration of Roman coins in Fife.

The *caer* element in the name 'Kirkcaldy' is perhaps a significant generic. It is now accepted that this element was originally Celtic, from the root 'enclose'—'field' or 'enclosure'. North of the Forth this *caer* element, however, occurs with remarkable frequency in relation to Roman forts.[5] As indicated, no forts and only a few temporary camps have been identified in mainland Fife. The *caer* element, however, may point to the existence of a Roman structure, however temporary, or a structure that was perceived to be Roman, in the Kirkcaldy area. The coin finds could, moreover, be indicative of a working relationship between the local population and the Romans rather than necessarily permanent Roman occupation. Aerial photography suggests a mass of small unenclosed settlements in this region of Fife and doubtless the Romans would take account of this native population, if only to keep a watchful eye on it, but also perhaps to forge trading links. It would appear that Kirkcaldy was used at least at times by the Romans, perhaps merely as a contact point between the indigenous people and themselves, or possibly as a port.[6]

the medieval and modern periods

Other than a few stray finds, discovered in the nineteenth century, all the archaeological work in Kirkcaldy has been carried out in the last three to four years. There has so far been no opportunity to examine the street frontages. All work has been concentrated in the backlands where evidence of garden soils and cultivation features has been found, indicating that the boundaries of the burgage plots extending back from the street frontages are still preserved, at least in places, on either side of the High Street. Small amounts of medieval pottery have been retrieved from each site, dating from the late fifteenth or the sixteenth centuries.

In a wider context, recent archaeological work has suggested that medieval settlement on the western side of the High Street was initially limited to a narrow strip alongside the street frontage, in marked contrast to the much longer burgage plots to the east of the High Street **figure 3**. This would imply that the parish church originally stood in isolation, outside and overlooking the core of the medieval burgh.[7]

The human remains, stone coffins and inscriptions found in the nineteenth century at various locations on the west side of the High Street may perhaps indicate the site of an as yet unknown religious house, but without an accurate location reference, little more can be said.[8]

12

Precisely where and when in the medieval period settlement first came to the place now known as 'Kirkcaldy' is not clear. The element *culdee* in the placename would perhaps suggest an old Celtic name of prehistoric origin. There is a tradition that the first site of human occupation was beside the narrow ravine through which the East Burn enters the sea.[9] This spot certainly offered some of the essentials for early settlement: fresh drinking water from the burn and ready access to the sea for fishing boats, which could be easily beached on the shelving sands. A further important factor for early settlers was protection, not only from animals but also from human predators. So it may be significant that this area is close by Dunnikier (now called Pathhead) since this name includes an element, *dun*, which suggests a fortification or fortified hill.[10]

The first documentary reference to Kirkcaldy comes in the reign of Malcolm III (1058–93), when the shire of Kirkcaldy was granted by the king to the church of Dunfermline. In 1127 and 1130 when David I was confirming the grants of his father, it is referred to as the 'schyre of Kircalethin' and 'schire of Kirkcaladinit', although the precise locations of this shire and site of Kirkcaldy are not specified.[11] An 1182 mention of Kirkcaldy as a 'villa' is the sole evidence that it was considered a town in the twelfth century.[12] By 1304, however, the abbey of Dunfermline was appealing to Edward I for a weekly market and an annual fair for Kirkcaldy, since, it was claimed, this town, given to the abbey by David I, was 'one of the most ancient of burghs'.[13] But it may be significant that, while granting the right to a market and fair, the king referred to Kirkcaldy as merely a 'manor'.[14] By the reign of Robert I (1306–29), however, Kirkcaldy was definitely recognised as a burgh dependent on Dunfermline Abbey, along with the three other regality burghs of Dunfermline: Dunfermline, Queensferry and Musselburgh.[15]

The elevation of a township to a burgh held potentially far-reaching implications. With burgh status came rights and privileges. Although early municipal records no longer exist for Kirkcaldy, it is known from national documentation, such as the *Leges Burgorum* or 'Laws of the Burghs', and the charters of other early Scottish burghs, that burghs in Scotland had a well-developed system of municipal government, sharing much in common not only with each other, but also with their counterparts in England, the Low Countries and France.[16]

Kirkcaldy, being a burgh dependent on the abbey of Dunfermline, had as its superior the abbot of Dunfermline. How far the abbot intervened in local affairs is now impossible to say, but the records of the burgh of Dunfermline, which begin in 1433,[17] suggest that there was no undue interference on the part of the abbot in municipal affairs in that burgh. Indeed, there appears to have been a genuine attempt at co-operation between town and superior for mutual benefit; it is not unreasonable to assume that the same was true for Kirkcaldy. The town's principal officers were the two bailies. Probably initially they were the nominees of the abbot, but in due course, as in other burghs, they doubtless came to represent the burgesses, or freemen of the burgh, more closely, although the interests of the abbot as burgh superior would always be borne in mind. In 1451 Kirkcaldy was granted feu-ferme status, which meant that the burgh was formally recognised as competent not only to handle the routine administration of the town, but also to control its own fiscal policy. By entering into an agreement with the abbot of Dunfermline to render annually 33s 4d, the community of the burgh gained authority over all their burgh revenues, such as burgh rents, multures and revenues from fishings. The great customs levied on exports alone were excluded. However, the abbot's right to reprimand the Kirkcaldy bailies in the event of misdemeanour was retained.[18]

By the time the Kirkcaldy Records become extant, in 1562,[19] there is evidence of a degree of self-determination in the town, at least for the burgesses, the only indwellers in the town with rights. They participated in the head courts of the burgh, which all burgesses were, officially, obliged to attend and where major policy decisions were taken. These were held either in the open air on the common muir, to the west of the town, or in the tolbooth, the most important civic building (*see* p 30). Routine administration was probably initially left to an assize of a few burgesses or a burgh court, since there is no evidence of a town council before 1582.[20] Nor did Kirkcaldy appoint a principal officer in the person of a provost, deciding at an assize in 1588 that it would be an 'inconvenience and danger' and bring 'servitude and slaverie' to the town.[21] A provost first appears in the Burgh Records in 1658, by which time Kirkcaldy had been confirmed as a royal burgh, in 1644.[22]

One of the most significant liberties, or privileges, granted with burgh status was the right to trade freely. It is not certain whether the permission given by Edward I in the early fourteenth century, to set up a market and fair in Kirkcaldy, was acted upon immediately. There is every likelihood, however, that from the reign of Robert I Kirkcaldy began to benefit, along with the three other regality burghs, from any trading concessions bestowed on the abbey of Dunfermline and its dependent burghs. During this reign, for example, in an undated charter the great customs of wool, skins and leather, which were normally reserved to the crown, were granted to the abbot and abbey of Dunfermline throughout its regality.[23] This would doubtless encourage trade within the regality, and it appears to have been confirmed in 1321. In that year the king advised the magistrates and community of Bruges of his intention to furnish the regality with a cocket, that is a seal, permitting custom-free export.[24] This would suggest that there was already a fair degree of trade in custumable goods between the regality burghs and the Low Countries.

Two further concessions were bestowed by the crown in 1363. The abbey and its burgesses and merchants were given a port at the grange of Gellet or West Rosyth. It is unlikely that this was of much advantage to any burgesses other than those of Dunfermline. The second grant, however, was highly significant for Kirkcaldy. The burgesses of the regality burghs were given the monopoly of buying and selling without payment of toll or tax within the bounds not only of their burghs but also throughout the entire regality.[25] This concession, allied with the cocket allowing trade with Bruges, may have been used over-enthusiastically, for in 1384 Robert II deemed that the privilege of custom-free export had been extended to goods produced outwith regality lands and an embargo was placed for a few years, and subsequently lifted, on exports from the regality.[26] The abbey's *Registrum de Dunfermlyn* and Dunfermline's burgh records indicate clearly that the regality north of the Forth was divided between Kirkcaldy and Dunfermline for trading purposes.[27] Although this at times led to dispute, for example in 1448 as to whether inhabitants of Goatmilk should go to Kirkcaldy's or Dunfermline's market, there is here clear evidence that Kirkcaldy's market was functioning effectively and that the burgh was determined to protect its trading rights.[28]

Kirkcaldy had significant advantages, being set on the east coast with close contacts with Scotland's main trading partners, the Low Countries, the Baltic region, England and northern France. How early its first harbour was built, to take advantage of its site, is not clear (*see* pp 53–6), but at least by 1451 there was a functioning harbour, however small, as it is referred to in the feu-ferme charter between the abbot of Dunfermline and the burgesses of Kirkcaldy.[29] The early sixteenth-century *Treasurer's Accounts* indicate that timber was imported, probably from the Baltic, to Kirkcaldy for use at both Falkland Palace and Edinburgh Castle, as well as for shipbuilding.[30] This import of wood, according to the *Exchequer Rolls*, was still flourishing at the end of the century.[31] Trade with England is also well evidenced, the *Bruce* of Kirkcaldy, for example, making regular visits to Boston, and the *Fortune* of Kirkcaldy carrying salt and the *Hope* of Kirkcaldy herring to London.[32] The message from the mayor of Cork to the burgesses of Kirkcaldy, in 1608, that one of Kirkcaldy's ships, the *Hert*, had been looted by pirates of her cargo of wheat, tallow, fish and yarn illustrates trading contacts with Ireland.[33] The Low Countries were also regularly visited by Kirkcaldy ships.[34] The commissioning of the king's page to purchase shirts in Kirkcaldy in 1546 is probably indication that luxury goods were passing through Kirkcaldy's port and market;[35] by 1619 the *Jennet* of Kirkcaldy was carrying hatbands embroidered in gold and silver.[36] The town's exports still consisted largely of raw materials, such as hides, wool and skins, and herring, salmon, coal and salt had already begun to figure prominently.

The importance to the community of sea-borne trade is reflected in the establishment of a 'Prime Gilt Box Fund' in 1591, for the support of sailors in need. All mariners on

14

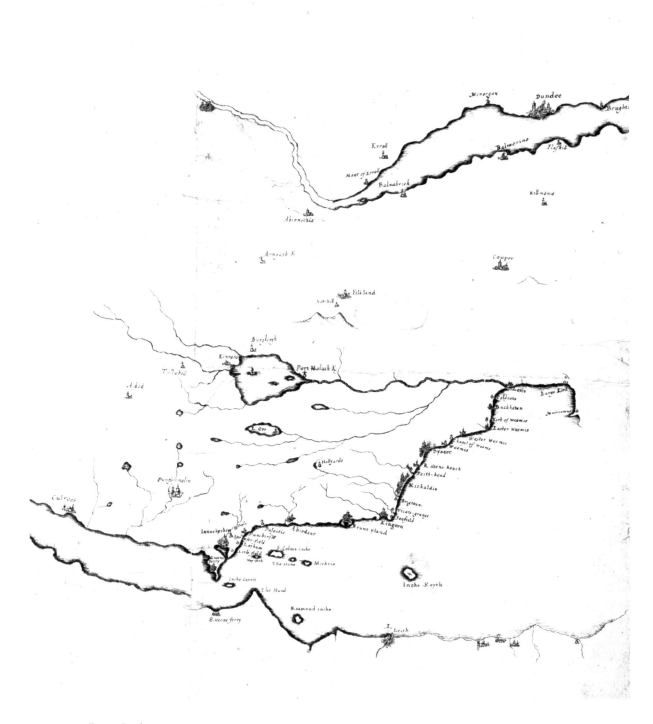

figure 5
Map of central
Scotland by Robert
Gordon of Straloch
c 1630 *National
Library of Scotland
map room*

return from a sea voyage were to place 2d into the fund; it was overseen by a box-master and thirteen key-holders. Perhaps even more telling was the care the townspeople took over their harbour. It had been said of Kirkcaldy in 1544 that it had a pier, a very good landing with boats at 'full see' and a good road within half a mile of the shore. In 1589, however, the 'haill commountie' convened in the kirk to lay down a scheme for building a totally new pier and harbour. In spite of financial problems and protracted negotiations, by 1600 repairs and alterations to the harbour were under way, and work on the new pier was so well advanced that the old one was totally dismantled and the wood laid aside, at the expense of the townspeople, for use elsewhere (*see* p 55). Clearly their sea-borne trade and harbour were of prime importance for such radical, and, for the time, unusual renewals to have been undertaken.[37]

Coarse cloth and nails produced in Kirkcaldy and Pathhead were the main manufactured products,[38] the nail industry supplying the royal Master of Works for repair work to Holyrood Palace into the seventeenth century.[39] Kirkcaldy's craftsmen were sufficiently skilled to be called upon to repair royal saddles.[40] Many of the locals must have found employment in the salt-pans and coal pits that are known to have been worked in the town's vicinity from at least the early sixteenth century.[41] Indeed, the Burgh Records of June 1582 referred to an 'old' act that insisted that all coal holes on the burgh muir should be filled in by midsummer, thus indicating workings close to the town precincts[42] **figure 19**. By the beginning of the 1570s Kirkcaldy had twenty-eight salt-pans, owned by seven different owners, second only to Prestonpans and Musselburgh, which had thirty-one pans between them **figure 19**. Kirkcaldy's production of salt was aided by the practice that arose of the salters effecting their own stonework repairs, rather than hiring the expensive services of a mason to repair roofs and hearths.[43]

Increased revenues that resulted from both internal and export trade, as well as the skills of craftsmen, meant that the burgh was stented for the first time in 1535 and represented at the Convention of Royal Burghs, along with Dunfermline, from 1574, even though neither was technically a royal burgh.[44] They were, however, of such importance economically that their presence was desirable, which probably also explains Kirkcaldy's admission to parliament in 1585.[45]

The increasing trade and prosperity of the burgh can, to a certain extent, be traced through the rise in its share of national burgh taxation in the century and a half after 1535: by 1635 it had increased from 0.7 per cent to 2.3 per cent and was ranked eighth; by 1683, when its assessment had risen to 3.2 per cent, it was ranked sixth. A steep fall in tax assessment, however, followed in the twenty years before the Union of 1707, reflecting the difficulties which the burgh and its port faced, particularly in the decline of its coal exporting trade.[46]

Once Kirkcaldy's own records become fuller, as they do in the last quarter of the sixteenth century, a clearer picture of the townscape emerges. The town was not large: it has been estimated that the population of the parish was around 3,000 to 3,200 in 1639 and that it was about 3,400 in 1691.[47] Its population may well have fallen during the first half of the eighteenth century; Webster's census of 1755 gave 2,296 parishioners in Kirkcaldy parish.[48] Yet early commentators speak of Kirkcaldy as one of the important burghs of Fife, Hector Boece, for example, classifying it, along with St Andrews, Dysart, Kinghorn, Cupar and Dunfermline, as a 'noble town'.[49] In the late seventeenth century, Daniel Defoe described Kirkcaldy as a 'larger, more populous, and better built town than … any on this coast' with one main street 'a long mile' in length[50] **figure 19**.

The town was essentially one long street. The configuration of the town had been largely determined by its geography, squeezed on a coastal plain between the sea and the Lomond foothills **figure 3**. Early maps show graphically that even in the sixteenth and seventeenth centuries Kirkcaldy was a 'lang toun' **figure 5**.

A back lane ran behind the burgage plots to the west of High Street from Kirk Wynd in a southerly direction. This would in due course become developed and be called Hill Street. Small closes and wynds entered the High Street, one of the most important being Kirk Wynd, at the top of which sat the parish church of St Bryce, overlooking the small

16

figure 6

'Kirkcaldy from the
north, 1838'
artist unknown
*Kirkcaldy Museum
and Art Gallery*

settlement. By the sixteenth century the main thoroughfare was paved, or cobbled, with
flags covering small burns that ran down the slope towards the sea across the High Street.
Wells stood in the street and in some closes. Running back from the main street, which
was paved by the time the records are extant, were the burgage plots, tofts or rigs, of the
townspeople. These narrow strips of land had on the frontage the houses of the burgesses,
with the rears, or backlands, being used to grow produce, contain animals and support
workshops, midden heaps and wells. On the sea side, plots ran down to the beach and
probably functioned as private beaching grounds for individual tenements. The other side
of the High Street had backlands rising steeply to the terracing of the Lomond foothills.
These latter rigs are clearly visible at the north end of High Street on nineteenth-century
views, and on the ground still to this day **figure 6**.

The town was not surrounded with a stone wall, a feature not common in Scotland. A
measure of protection, however, was afforded by the natural defence of the sea, although
this did leave the town open to potential sea-borne attack. The building of Ravenscraig
Castle to the north of the town in 1460–4 (*see* pp 64–5) reduced this danger. At the foot of
the rigs to the west of High Street burgesses placed small walls or 'heid dykes', which
afforded a measure of protection from outsiders. Most of these dykes had small gates,
allowing the burgesses access to the countryside and the town crofts, where produce was
grown and animals grazed. It was the responsibility of the burgesses to maintain these
dykes and gates in good order, and to ensure that strangers did not enter, particularly in
time of plague.[51] In 1585, a plague year, it was enacted that 'all enteress at venelis, bak
syddis and bak yairdis be stoppit and maid fast be the awneris and na strangearis to be
ressavit in nor out thairatt'.[52] Such measures were not always successful. It is estimated
that perhaps three hundred people died in Kirkcaldy during this outbreak, and a
Kirkcaldy resident was blamed for carrying the infection to Leith.[53]

Three main gates or ports were the official entry points to the burgh. The East Port
stood to the north end of the town, another was sited near the parish church in Kirk
Wynd, and a third, the West Port, controlled the southern approach to the town and,
along with the Kirk Wynd port, gave access to the nearby common muir. The ports were
more of a psychological barrier between the town and outsiders than genuinely defensive,
but the town was expected to maintain a modicum of self-protection. In 1533, according
to the *Treasurer's Accounts*, Kirkcaldy was instructed to hold a 'wappinshaw', or weapon
inspection of burgesses, and to have 'bulwerkis and defenssis maid'.[54] Twenty-five years
later, the people of Kirkcaldy, along with other burghs, were to 'big dikis and fowseis' and
'have staff slungis [slings with cords attached to staffs] in the reddines to the portis
thereof'.[55]

The ports had other functions too. All those entering the town to use the burgh market
paid tolls at the ports or at the tolbooth. The ports were also closed at night after curfew

to prevent unchecked entry and exit, and shut to all outsiders during the time of plague. In the 1585 plague scare, all strangers wishing access were channelled through the East Port for scrutiny.[56] The fact that settlement had stretched beyond the East Port to the harbour by the sixteenth century is clear indication of the importance of the harbour and its environs to the townspeople. The site of the port is probably an indication of the extent of the burgh in previous centuries.[57]

The dwellings that fronted the High Street would mostly have been relatively simple structures in the late sixteenth century, largely constructed of wood, or even of wattle and daub. Some of these were in due course replaced by more prestigious buildings to house the wealthier merchants and craftsmen of the town, as may still be witnessed in a few standing buildings (*see* pp 61–5) **figures 13**, **14** *&* **16**. An analysis of the hearth tax returns of 1691 confirms this impression. Kirkcaldy had a larger proportion of households with four or more hearths, which accommodated local lairds, merchants and maltmen, than burghs of a similar size, such as Dumfries and Linlithgow—78 out of a total of 509 houses in the burgh. For a town of this size there were also, by contrast, rather fewer single hearths than might usually be expected: the 297 in Kirkcaldy accounted for some 58 per cent of all households, whereas in Dumfries the same figure was 63 per cent and in Linlithgow 69 per cent. It is a striking commentary on Kirkcaldy's wealth and trade before the slippage which took place early in the eighteenth century that, in 1691, over six out of every ten houses in the burgh had at least two rooms, each with a hearth in it.[58]

Demand for extra living space in a confined site led to encroachment onto the High Street by extensions such as wooden booths and forestairs, thus narrowing the thoroughfare. The gaoling of two people in 1661 for building a forestair to a building on the High Street and consequently blocking three of a neighbour's windows was not unusual. Given that the main street was only 14 feet (4.25 m) broad in 1582, reduced in places to as little as 11 feet 9 inches (3.5 m) by 1809, space was highly restricted.[59] By the eighteenth century the front walls of a number of the houses were rebuilt with strong beams in the ceiling, so permitting a new front wall to be constructed further into the street. By 1792 the High Street houses were described as 'mean, awkwardly placed, with their ends to the street', such had been the encroachment into the street.[60]

Kirkcaldy's modest prosperity was to suffer setbacks during the political crises of the seventeenth century. The National Covenant was subscribed in the town in 1638; two years later the bailies of the burgh decreed that all burgesses were to receive military training. The elder of the Kirkcaldy presbytery, General Leslie, was appointed commander of the Scots army, which may have encouraged local support for the Covenanting cause.[61] The magistrates and council conferred the freedom of the burgh on eighty volunteers who took up arms. Kirkcaldy, however, lost several hundred (tradition claims the number to be 480) men in the Covenanting wars; many of its trading vessels were destroyed or taken; and the town's treasures, sent to Dundee for safe-keeping, were seized by General Monck in 1651.

The scale of the devastation brought about during the 1640s and 1650s is uncertain. In 1668, it was reported that 'almost all the ships and vessels belonging to H M subjects of Scotland were during the last usurpation taken brunt or destroyed' and there is a tradition that Kirkcaldy lost ninety-four ships between 1644 and 1660.[62] Whether or not this particular claim was exaggerated, there is little doubt that the town's losses were extensive. Between 1640 and 1644 approximately a hundred ships were registered in Kirkcaldy, although not all were Kirkcaldy-owned as Kirkcaldy was the registration port for all the burghs between Aberdour and Crail. By 1650 twenty-six ships appear on the register, and by 1656 only twelve. The period of the Cromwellian occupation brought its own pressures; in 1655, when Cromwell lodged at Ravenscraig Castle, his troops were billeted on the townspeople, and their horses, according to local tradition, stabled in the parish church.[63] When Thomas Tucker, a commissioner of the Commonwealth government, visited the burgh in the following year he found Kirkcaldy, along with others, 'pitiful small townes ... inhabited by seamen, colliers, salt makers and such like people'.[64] There is also evidence, however, that by this time Kirkcaldy's craftsmen included hammermen, wrights, cordiners, tailors, baxters, fleshers, weavers, masons, candlemakers, brewers, maltmen and coopers.[65] As well as the coal heughs, stone and lime quarries were being worked;[66] and the frequent attempts of the Kirkcaldy presbytery in the 1640s to halt Sunday workings at the salt-pans indicates a thriving salt industry.[67]

Efforts were made to effect a recovery after 1660, although the Restoration period also saw more demands made by the military; the town was again used as a billet in 1663 and 1689. In an attempt to aid recovery of shipping, it was decided in 1662 that no-one should be admitted as burgess unless he had first expended 500 merks (£333 13s 4d) on a ship or share of one. This may have met with some success as twenty-five ships appear on the register in 1673. By 1682, however, the burgh was petitioning the Convention of Royal Burghs against its tax assessment, with little success, as a further 2,000 merks was added to its stent.[68] Six years later, in a further appeal, perhaps exaggerated, it was claimed that trade was decayed, ships and men lost, and that both magistrates and ordinary inhabitants were abandoning the town, such was the distress.[69] An application for support to William and Mary in 1689 may be a reflection of genuine hardship. The *Register* containing information on the state of every burgh in 1692 certainly paints a gloomy picture of Kirkcaldy. Nineteen ships had been lost in the previous ten years, leaving only four ferry boats and fourteen ships with an average age of twenty years,[70] a ship being considered well past its prime at this age.[71]

By the turn of the century, there was little evidence of improvement economically. Crail, Kilrenny, the two Anstruthers and Pittenweem, all fishing towns, along with Dysart, Kirkcaldy, Kinghorn and Burntisland, coal and salt towns primarily, by 1705 together paid only 2.85 per cent of the tax roll, a decline to one third of their assessment in 1612.[72] The Union of 1707 brought further hardship to Scottish ports, Kirkcaldy included, although there is some evidence that between 1719 and 1721 the heavy losses faced by the town with a drop in coal sales were more than compensated for by large profits from the salt trade.[73] Heavy customs and excise dues, however, designed to equalise dues within Great Britain, resulted, for Kirkcaldy, in a steep decline in shipping. By 1760 only three ships, manned by a total of eleven men, were registered as using Kirkcaldy harbour.[74] One was a coaster, and the other two were ferry boats plying between Kirkcaldy and Newhaven. For much of the first three-quarters of the century the harbour was in a ruinous state (*see* p 56).

Manufacturing, however, was to transform Kirkcaldy's fortunes. Linen weaving, said to have started in the town in 1672,[75] became one of the town's mainstays, with yarn being imported from Hamburg and Bremen.[76] By 1733 almost 180,000 yards were produced

figure 7

View of the harbour in the nineteenth century
Kirkcaldy Museum and Art Gallery

annually and this was to double in the next three years.[77] Demand was such that an annual linen market was held from 1739.[78] By 1743 cloth to the value of £11,000 was woven in Kirkcaldy and this had increased to £22,000 by 1755.[79] In 1751 a market specifically for lint seed was set up to encourage the local growing of flax.[80] There is a local tradition that Kirkcaldy was the first Scottish town to use the power loom, in 1821.[81] Cotton spinning also supplemented the traditional local industries of coal mining and salt-panning and boosted Kirkcaldy's trade with the Baltic and the Low Countries.[82] There is evidence that the loss of overseas trade in salt was more than compensated for as the century progressed by the rapid increase in the home market.[83]

The general increase in overseas trade was reflected in the numbers of ships registered: seven ships with total crews of fifty men in 1782 increased to twenty-nine ships with 225 men in 1792. According to the burgh records of Glasgow, Kirkcaldy was one of only four ports on the Forth, the others being Leith, Alloa and Dunbar (with Bo'ness not being classified as an eastern port), importing grain from the Baltic.[84] A further boost to the local economy came with the establishment of shipbuilding in the town. Thirty-eight vessels were built in the fifteen years after its commencement in 1778, most destined for Forth ports, but some for Glasgow, Dundee and Aberdeen, and one for New Zealand.[85] Brewing, distilling, ironfounding, as well as a flourishing corn and meal trade and whaling, also brought employment and prosperity to the town. By 1790 it was further benefiting from the High Street becoming part of the route of the new turnpike road from Pettycur to Newport-on-Tay, via Cupar.[86]

In 1831 Kirkcaldy was described as 'the most thriving town on the north coast of the Firth of Forth'.[87] This was reflected in its public buildings—banks, schools, churches, libraries, in a style indicative of the prosperous new era (*see* pp 63–4)—and in widened and repaved streets.[88] With this, however, came an increasingly industrialised townscape, served by a new railway system connecting to the harbour by 1849[89] **figure 7**. The traditional manufactories were to benefit significantly from this development, in particular the coal industry which had suffered from heavy carriage expenses—a ton of coal, for example, costing 4s to cover the four miles from Clunie to Kirkcaldy in the mid-1790s.[90] In 1847 Michael Nairn opened his first factory, at Pathhead, known initially as 'Nairn's Folly', for making floor-cloth 'according to the most approved methods then practised'. By 1883 floor-cloth and linoleum were made in seven factories in Kirkcaldy and employed 1,300, thus setting in train Kirkcaldy's important linoleum export trade.[91] Linen manufacturing also prospered in the 1860s, with, by 1867, eighteen factories employing 3,887 people.[92]

The expansion of the town was such that by 1876 Kirkcaldy burgh assimilated its smaller neighbouring burghs, Linktown, Pathhead and Sinclairtown, as well as Invertiel and Gallatown. Prosperity and industrialisation launched the wealthier classes out into more salubrious new suburbs, leaving the old town centre to decline to a slum area. Much of the old High Street, however, remained intact, albeit in a decayed state, until the redevelopment of the 1960s and 1970s, which left only a few standing buildings and an unknown archaeological potential as testament to Kirkcaldy's historic past.

notes

1   T Darvill, *Prehistoric Britain* (London, 1987), 103.

2   D Breeze, *The Northern Frontiers of Roman Britain* (London, 1982), 132.

3   G Maxwell, *The Romans in Scotland* (Edinburgh, 1989), 124.

4   *Ibid*, 124–6.

5   Personal comment, Mr Simon Taylor, School of Scottish Studies, University of Edinburgh. We are indebted to Simon Taylor for his

views and assistance with these points.

6   Personal comment, Dr Gordon Maxwell, Royal Commission on Ancient and Historical Monuments. We are indebted to Dr Maxwell for his assistance.

7   SUAT, 'Trial Excavations at Seaview House, Oswald's Wynd, Kirkcaldy' (1994, unpublished).

20

8   *NSA*, ix, 748.

9   J Campbell, A T Richardson, G MacGregor, G Deas & L Macbean, *Kirkcaldy Burgh and Schyre: Landmarks of Local History* (Kirkcaldy, 1924), 80.

10   Personal comment, Simon Taylor. For alternative views on the placename evidence, *see* E Eunson, *Bygone Fife* (Glasgow, 1910), 1; P K Livingstone, *A History of Kirkcaldy, 1843–1949* (Kirkcaldy, 1955), 9.

11   *Dunf Reg*, nos 1, 2.

12   *Ibid*, no 238.

13   *CDS*, ii, no 1624.

14   *Ibid*, no 1653.

15   *Dunf Reg*, no 346.

16   *Leges Burgorum*, reputedly of the reign of David I (1124–53); statutes from the time of William the Lion (1165–1214); *Statute Gilde*, a set of rulings promulgated in Berwick in the latter half of the thirteenth century. M Bateson (ed), *Borough Customs*, 2 vols (Selden Soc, 1904); A Ballard & J Tait (edd), *British Borough Charters, 1216–1307* (Cambridge, 1923).

17   E P Dennison Torrie (ed), *The Gild Court Book of Dunfermline, 1433–1597* (Scottish Record Society, 1986); *Dunf Recs*.

18   *Dunf Reg*, no 432.

19   *KBR*.

20   *KBR*, 71.

21   *KBR*, 118.

22   *KBR*, 168; G S Pryde, *The Burghs of Scotland* (Oxford, 1965), no 78.

23   *RMS*, i, 24; *Dunf Reg*, no 346.

24   *Dunf Reg*, no 361.

25   *Dunf Reg*, nos 390 (appendix i), 391 (appendix ii).

26   *Dunf Reg*, no 394.

27   E P Dennison Torrie, 'The Gild of Dunfermline in the Fifteenth Century' (University of Edinburgh PhD thesis, 1984), 236; *cf* J M Webster & A A M Duncan (edd), *The Regality of Dunfermline Court Book* (Dunfermline, 1953), 25.

28   Torrie (ed), *Dunfermline Gild Court Book*, fo 104v.

29   *Dunf Reg*, no 432.

30   *TA*, ii, 278, 279; iv, 97, 458; viii, 169, 372. *See also* J Dow, '*Skotter* in sixteenth-century Scania', *Scottish Historical Review*, xliv (1965), 36.

31   *ER*, xxiii, 319. *See also* J Dow, 'Scottish trade with Sweden,1512–80', *Scottish Historical Review*, xlix (1969), 65.

32   S G E Lythe, *The Economy of Scotland in its European Setting, 1550–1625* (Edinburgh, 1960), 135, 217, 218.

33   *Ibid*, 137.

34   *Ibid*, 244.

35   *TA*, viii, 473.

36   Lythe, *Economy of Scotland*, 225.

37   J Y Lockhart, *Kirkcaldy Burgh and Harbour: An Historical Outline* (Kirkcaldy, 1940), 2; J Bain (ed), *The Hamilton Papers: Letters and Papers Illustrating the Political Relations of England and Scotland in the Sixteenth Century*, 2 vols (Edinburgh, 1892), ii, 714.

38   *ER*, xxii, 94, for example.

39   *Accounts of the Master of Works for Buildings and Repairing Royal Palaces and Castles*, edd H M Paton *et al*, 2 vols (Edinburgh, 1957–82), i, 321.

40   *TA*, vi, 421.

41   *RMS*, iii, no 2138; *RPC*, ii, 265, 427; *Dunf Reg*, appendix ii, 433, 462.

42   *KBR*, 70.

43   C A Whatley, *The Scottish Salt Industry, 1570–1850* (Aberdeen, 1987), 20, 69, 33.

44   *RCRB*, i, 515, 25.

45   *APS*, iii, 423.

46   M Lynch, 'Continuity and change in urban society, 1500–1700', in R A Houston & I D Whyte (edd), *Scottish Society, 1500–1800* (Cambridge, 1989), 115; T C Smout, *Scottish Trade on the Eve of Union, 1660–1707* (Edinburgh, 1963), 282–3.

47   I D Whyte, 'Urbanization in early-modern Scotland: a preliminary analysis', *Scottish Economic and Social History*, ix (1989), 24; M Lynch, 'Urbanisation and urban networks in seventeenth-century Scotland: some further thoughts', *Scottish Economic and Social History*, xii (1992), 1–21.

48   'Webster's Analysis of Population', in *Scottish Population Statistics* (SHS, 1952), pp. xliv, 40.

49   P Hume Brown (ed), *Scotland before 1700 from Contemporary Documents* (Edinburgh, 1893), 78.

50 D Defoe, *A Tour Through the Whole Island of Great Britain*, edd P Furbank & W R Owens (London, 1991; orig pub 1724), 346.

51 MS Kirkcaldy Burgh Court Book, 18 January 1602, and 10 October 1604, for example.

52 *KBR*, 107.

53 Lythe, *Economy of Scotland*, 18.

54 *TA*, vi, 129.

55 *TA*, x, 336.

56 *KBR*, 107.

57 MS Kirkcaldy Burgh Records, 12 October 1584.

58 SRO, E69/10/2 (Hearth Tax records); *West Lothian Hearth Tax, 1691*, ed D Adamson (Scottish Record Society, 1981), 92–4. Kirkcaldy had a total of 509 households: 297 had single hearths (58.4%); 89 had two hearths (17.5%); 45 had three hearths (8.8%); and 78 (15.3%) had four hearths or more. For Linlithgow and Dumfries, which had 10% and 7% of their houses with four or more hearths respectively, *see* D Adamson, 'The hearth tax', *Transactions of Dumfriesshire and Galloway Natural History and Antiquarian Society*, 3rd ser, xlvii (1970–71), 147–77, esp 149. The Kirkcaldy hearth tax record, unfortunately, makes no distinctions as to quarters of the burgh or any other internal boundaries.

59 *KBR*, 70; *RPC*, 3rd ser, i, 47; Richard Moore, 'Map of the Burgh of Kirkcaldy' (1809).

60 *OSA*, x, 507.

61 Kirkcaldy's seventeenth-century MS Presbytery Records reveal consistent attempts to raise funds for the Covenanting military cause.

62 Smout, *Scottish Trade*, 240, citing *Calendar of State Papers, Domestic, Charles II*, vol ccxxxiii, 14, and H Farnie, *The Handy Book of the Fife Coast* (n d), 45.

63 Campbell *et al*, *Kirkcaldy Burgh and Schyre*, 51–2.

64 P Hume Brown (ed), *Early Travellers in Scotland* (Edinburgh, 1891), 169.

65 Kirkcaldy District Archive, MS 1.9.5; *KBR*, 169, 177, 182.

66 *Ibid*, 335; *APS*, viii, 139.

67 Whatley, *Scottish Salt Industry*, 40.

68 Campbell *et al*, *Kirkcaldy Burgh and Schyre*, 169.

69 F H Groome, *Ordnance Gazetteer of Scotland: A Survey of Scottish Topography*, 6 vols (Edinburgh, 1886), iv, 415.

70 'Register containing the state and condition of every burgh within the kingdom of Scotland in the year 1692', in *Scottish Burgh Records Society Miscellany* (1881), 83–5.

71 Smout, *Scottish Trade*, 51.

72 *Ibid*, 136.

73 Whatley, *Scottish Salt Industry*, 65.

74 Lockhart, *Kirkcaldy Burgh and Harbour, passim*.

75 Groome, *Ordnance Gazetteer*, iv, 414.

76 *KBR*, 239, 263; *OSA*, x, 535.

77 Groome, *Ordnance Gazetteer*, iv, 414.

78 Richard Pococke, *Tours in Scotland, 1747, 1750, 1760*, ed D W Kemp (SHS, 1887), 281.

79 Groome, *Ordnance Gazetteer*, iv, 414.

80 Campbell *et al*, *Kirkcaldy Burgh and Schyre*, 56.

81 R Heron, *Scotland Delineated* (Edinburgh, 1975; orig pub 1799), 174.

82 J M Pearson, *Around Kirkcaldy* (Kirkcaldy, 1993), 13.

83 Whatley, *Scottish Salt Industry, 50*.

84 *Extracts from the Burgh Records of Glasgow*, 11 vols, edd J D Marwick & R Renwick (Scottish Burgh Records Soc & Glasgow, 1876–1916), ix, 1.

85 Lockhart, *Kirkcaldy Burgh and Harbour, passim*; Defoe, *Tour*, 346.

86 Eunson, *Bygone Kirkcaldy*, 3.

87 *Report on the Burgh of Kirkcaldy, Fifeshire, to Accompany the Reform Act of 1832* (Historical Discovery, Crewe, n d).

88 Groome, *Ordnance Gazetteer*, iv, 414.

89 Lockhart, *Kirkcaldy Burgh and Harbour*, 1.

90 B F Duckham, *A History of the Scottish Coal Industry*, vol i (Newton Abbot, 1970), 209.

91 Groome, *Ordnance Gazetteer*, iv, 415.

92 *Ibid*, iv, 414.

summary of previous archaeological work and chance finds

prehistoric and Roman

Invertiel Bridge NT 276 901
Polished stone axe.

Glamis Road NT 257 932
Polished stone axe.

polished stone axes NT 27 91
Two axes found in 1882, formerly in collection of Sir John Evans, now in Ashmolean Museum, Oxford. J Evans, *The Ancient Stone Implements, Weapons and Ornaments of Great Britain*, 2nd edn. (London, 1897).

Port Brae NT 283 917
Macehead Perforated stone macehead, found at Port Brae and donated to Kirkcaldy Museum.

Whytehouse Mansions NT 279 912
Stone axe Perforated stone axe, donated to Kirkcaldy Museum

Raith Park NT 261 914
Cup and ring-marked stone Built into the original boundary wall of the old Raith Estate Gardens is a cup and ring-marked stone. *DES* (1987), 12.

• *Priory Park NT 2837 9235*
Cist A cist burial comprising four side slabs with a covering lid was discovered during the digging of foundation trenches for a housing development. The foot stone appeared to have been dressed. The inhumation was laid on a bed of small, rounded pebbles (*see* **figure 4**). There was no evidence of any grave goods but fragments of calcined animal bone were found near the chest. Examination of the skeleton revealed the burial to be of a young female, aged between 25 and 30, with some bones showing signs of repetitive strain injuries. *DES* (1992), 30.

• *High Street NT 281 916*
Cists Demolition and foundation clearance revealed the remains of three cists. One cist, set in pure sand, was almost completely destroyed. The other two were partly preserved in the cement of the house foundations, and contained inhumed remains, which showed traces of burning. One of these burials had a food vessel, flint arrowhead and flint knife in association. *DES* (1980), 5.

• *Co-operative Store NT 27 91*
Cists Four 'stone coffins' were found in the excavations for the Co-operative store at Kirkcaldy. On top of one of them was an earthen urn. 'Miscellanea', *The Antiquary*, ii (1872), 232.

• *Braehead no NGR*
Cist Cist with food vessel found at Braehead. V G. Childe, *Scotland before the Scots* (Edinburgh, 1946), 114.

• *Oriel Road, NT 2721 9164*
Cists Two short cist burials were revealed during excavations in 1931 for a new slaughterhouse in Oriel Road. One cist contained a beaker, a wooden-hafted tanged bronze blade, a possible bronze pin, a flint flake, a dozen conical buttons, a jet bead and a probably

female skeleton. The other contained a male skeleton and a bone-hafted knife-dagger in a   23
leather sheaf of a type to be assigned to the end of the beaker period or the food vessel
period. The beaker, beads and bronze dagger are in Kirkcaldy Museum (the abattoir is
shown on OS. 25" map 1938, at NO 2721 9164). *PSAS*, lxxviii (1943–4), 109–14.

Roman Camp NT 284 947
Supposed site of Roman Camp at Carberry Farm. No physical remains survive.

13 Ravenscraig Street NT 2927 9267 – 2921 9281
Roman coin A slightly worn Antoninianus of Postumus (260–269) was found at a depth of
18" in a garden at 13 Ravenscraig Street. It was presented to Kirkcaldy Museum in 1959.
A S. Robertson, 'Roman coins in Scotland', *PSAS*, xciv (1960–1), 142.

East Smeaton Street NT 280 924
Roman coin A bronze coin of Constantine I (306–337) was found under two feet of soil at
East Smeaton Street in March 1965. A S Robertson, 'Roman coins in Scotland', *PSAS*, ciii
(1970–1), 122.

Roman coin NT 291 929
A bronze coin of Constans (337–350) was found in 1978 during maintenance of the
railway line in Kirkcaldy. A S Robertson, 'Roman coins in Scotland', *PSAS*, cxiii (1983),
412.

Dallas Drive, Templehall NT 260 933
Roman coin A bronze coin of Justin I was dug up in garden in Dallas Drive in 1966. A S
Robertson, 'Roman coins', *PSAS*, ciii (1970–1), 122.

Lennie's Yard, Gallatown no NGR
Roman coin Bronze coin of Constantius II (337–361), minted at Cyzicus, found in 1960, at
Lennie's Yard. A S Robertson, 'Roman coins', *PSAS*, ciii (1970–1), 122.

Roman coin NT 27 91
A fairly worn sestertius of Antoninus Pius (138–161) was found on a cart road in Kirkcaldy
c 1936. It was donated to Kirkcaldy Public Library. A S Robertson, 'Roman coins', *PSAS*,
xciv (1960–1), 141–2.

Roman coin NT 27 91
A fairly worn denarius of Lucius Verus (161–169), from Kirkcaldy, was brought to
Kirkcaldy Public Library. A S Robertson, 'Roman coins', *PSAS*, xciv (1960–1), 142.

Roman coins NT 27 91
Two bronze coins, one of Constantine II Caesar (337–361), and the other of Constantius
Gallus (421), were found while drains were being opened in Kirkcaldy. They were donated
to Kirkcaldy Public Library. A S Robertson, 'Roman coins', *PSAS*, xciv (1960–1), 142.

medieval

15 The Esplanade NT 282 916
Medieval garden soil and cultivation features Trial excavations on an extensive development site
produced evidence of nineteenth-century wall foundations and two possibly medieval
cultivation beds. *DES* (1993), 28.

High Street NT 2791 9101–2832 9177
Stone coffins Stone coffins and large quantities of human bones have been discovered in
different places along the High Street by workmen digging for foundations, and suggest
the presence of a religious house in the vicinity. *NSA*, ix, 748.

113 High Street NT 280 914

Medieval garden soil A watching brief was carried out in April 1993 on the insertion of a new pipe trench to the rear of the property at 113 High Street. Sealing the natural, 0.75 m below the ground level, was a 0.40 m thick sandy clay layer, a possible medieval garden soil, which produced a single sherd of late medieval pottery. A series of flagstones above the garden soil may have formed a yard surface, of Victorian or later date. SUAT Archive Report (1994, unpublished).

Seaview House, Oswald's Wynd/Church Lane NT 2815 9173

Medieval cultivation features An assessment was carried out in June 1994 in the walled garden of a nineteenth-century house, where it was proposed to construct a block of thirty-two flats and associated car parking facilities. A series of five trenches was opened by mechanical excavator across the site. A series of at least three well-defined terraces could be seen, cut into the slope of the hill.

The trenches revealed an accumulation of primarily eighteenth- and nineteenth-century garden soils, ranging in depth from 1 m at the west end to over 2 m at the east end. The terraces were of the same date, and traces of possible ornamental garden features were identified. Furrows in the natural sand in one of the trenches were sealed by a layer containing a seventeenth-century clay pipe; they may therefore indicate late medieval cultivation. Only one sherd of pottery, dating from the late fifteenth or sixteenth centuries, from a possible pit or gully, was recovered. SUAT Archive Report (1994, unpublished).

National Floorcloth Works NT 2769 9186

Quernstone The topstone of a quern, found in digging the foundation of the National Floorcloth Works, Kirkcaldy, was donated to the National Museum of Antiquities of Scotland (NMAS), Edinburgh (1870). Upper quernstone of yellow sandstone, 16", diameter imperfect. *PSAS*, viii (1868–70), 45 (Donations).

High Street, Nairn Street, Mitchell Place and Bogies Wynd NT 287 924

Medieval pottery sherd A pre-development watching brief was carried out in June 1990 on the site of a former linoleum works. The proximity of the site to Old Dunnikier House (Path House) suggested that other late medieval buildings may once have been present in the area. No evidence of any archaeological features survived, but two sherds of medieval pottery were retrieved from the spoil. *DES* (1990), 13.

area by area assessment

pp 26–60

historic buildings

pp 61–5

26

figure 8

Area location map

The medieval core of the town has been divided into six areas **figure 8**: two to the east of the High Street (Areas 1 and 2), three to the west (Areas 3, 4 and 5) and one at the north end of the High Street, incorporating the harbour (Area 6).

The sea provides an easily recognisable eastern limit to the development of the medieval town. The western limit, however, is rather more difficult to identify. Therefore, the areas to the west of the High Street are more arbitrary in their definition. In particular, Hill Street has been incorporated into two areas (3 and 4).

As the High Street forms the central division between Areas 1 and 2 to the east, and Areas 3, 4 and 5 to the west, each area overlaps to a certain extent to take in the frontage on the opposite side of the street. This ensures that important features of the medieval townscape, such as the town ports and market cross which were situated in the middle of the street, are not lost in the division between two areas.

area 1
Port Brae to Tolbooth Street / High Street / sea **figure 9**

description

This area is defined by High Street to the west, the Esplanade to the east, and Port Brae and Tolbooth Street, to the north and south respectively. Redburn Wynd and Adam Smith Close neatly sub-divide the area into three smaller areas.

At the north end, the area between Redburn Wynd and Port Brae is largely developed, with only small parcels of open ground in the south-east corner, used mainly for office parking.

The central block, between Adam Smith Close and Redburn Wynd, still reflects the character of the old medieval property divisions, with long, narrow, predominantly open plots extending from the High Street frontage down to the modern Esplanade.

The south end of this area, between Tolbooth Street and Adam Smith Close, again reflects the medieval pattern of property divisions. The majority of the plots are open, waste ground currently used as temporary or office car parking. A study of both the Moore (1809) and Wood (1824) maps shows a number of buildings attached directly onto what must have been surviving medieval or late medieval property boundaries **figure 19**. Many of these eighteenth- or nineteenth-century buildings have since been demolished or partially demolished, resulting in a series of up-standing walls, forming irregular and rather haphazardly shaped plots. One plot in particular is of interest here **G**, situated immediately to the south of Adam Smith Close, and east of 218 and 222 High Street. Although both the High Street and the Esplanade frontages of this plot have since been developed, the area between appears, from a visual examination, to be an overgrown garden, and seems to have escaped any significant development.

historical background

This area incorporates the northern end of the medieval burgh, its limit at one time demarcated by the East Port **A**. Precisely where this port stood is not known, but it can safely be assumed to have been in the area now called Port Brae.

previous archaeological work

15 The Esplanade NT 282 916 **E**

Three phases of archaeological trial work were carried out in late 1993 and early 1994, in advance of a development at 15 The Esplanade. The site, some 2,250 square metres, was

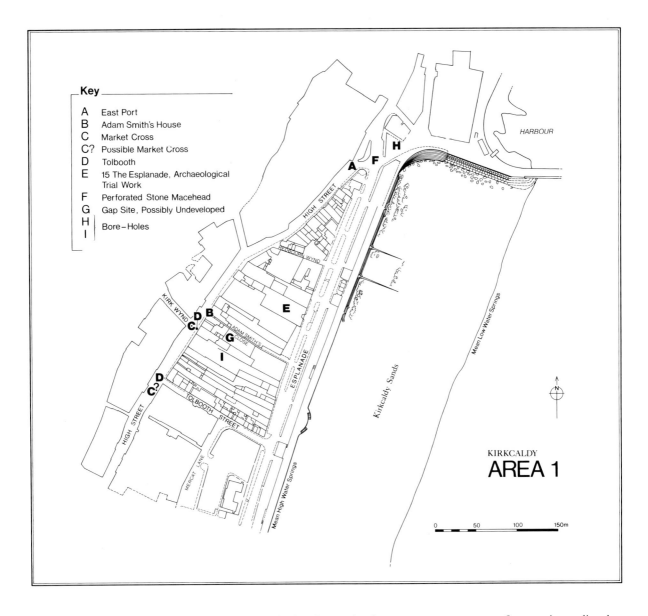

Key

A   East Port
B   Adam Smith's House
C   Market Cross
C? Possible Market Cross
D   Tolbooth
E   15 The Esplanade, Archaeological
    Trial Work
F   Perforated Stone Macehead
G   Gap Site, Possibly Undeveloped
H
I   Bore–Holes

KIRKCALDY
AREA 1

0   50   100   150m

figure 9

Area 1

history

Ports, or gates, usually simple wooden barresses, were common features in medieval burghs. Their primary function was to monitor access to the burgh. This included controlling entrance to the burgh market, the use of which demanded the payment of a toll, or tax, at the port or at the tolbooth (*see* p 30), and excluding potential carriers of plague during outbreaks of the 'pestilence' or 'pest'. In 1585, during a plague scare, it was decided that, apart from parishioners who were permitted to enter the burgh at the Kirk Wynd Port, all strangers were to be denied access by the West Port and were to approach

archaeology

situated in the High Street backlands, and between Redburn Wynd and Adam Smith Close, to the north and south respectively.

In the north and north-east part of the site, several walls were uncovered, one of which was associated with a stair tower, and stood to a height of *c* 1.8 m. Roofing material, within the demolition rubble that had accumulated against the walls, suggests that these were eighteenth or early nineteenth century in date, and, therefore, probably represent those buildings depicted on Moore's map of 1809 and Wood's map of 1824 **figure 19**.

In the south part of the site, two linear features, filled with garden soil, were revealed cut into the natural sand. The smaller of the two, measuring *c* 2.8 m in length and cut to a depth of 0.40 m, contained shell, charcoal, mortar and lenses of sand. The larger, measuring at least 5 m in length and cut to a depth of 0.50 m, produced one sherd of medieval pottery. Three large boulders were set into the sand, in the gap between the two features. These features are interpreted as possible cultivation beds, perhaps medieval in date. The boulders therefore may represent clearance. *DES* (1993), 28.

the town by the East Port for scrutiny.[1] Ports were usually set in walls surrounding the town, but most Scottish burghs, Kirkcaldy included, did not have stone encircling walls, relying for a measure of security on small, probably wooden, fences at the end of burgage plots. In all probability, although to date there is no evidence, a simple dyke passed from the shore to the East Port, and from there to the rear of the burgage plots to the west of High Street. There is no evidence, archaeological or documentary, of ditching, as is found in some burghs.

Redburn Wynd ran east-west some short distance to the south of Port Brae. It was sited beside the burn of the same name. Although traditionally so named after 'red', 'raid' or sewage, this was one of Kirkcaldy's important water supplies. There were, therefore, stringent rulings concerning the maintenance of its cleanliness. The fact that they were frequently repeated suggests, however, as does the name of the burn, that such rulings were not always obeyed. It was enacted, for example, at a head court of the burgh in 1593 that no one should bleach cloth on the side of the Red Burn;[2] eight years later it was considered of sufficient importance that, when it was ordered that no fish should be washed in the town's common burns, an inspector was assigned to the Red Burn.[3] Running as it did through a central area of the town, and crossing the High Street, it was flagged in places; the earliest evidence of this found to date is 1605.[4]

Further south, a pend at 220 High Street **B** is the site of the house where Adam Smith, the economist (1723–90), lived with his mother. It was here in 1767–76 that he completed *The Wealth of Nations*. This famous son of Kirkcaldy is portrayed on the Kirkcaldy Penny **front cover**.

Near to this site, in the middle of the High Street, at the bottom of Kirk Wynd, is one of the possible sites of the town's market cross **C**,[5] an alternative site being further south down the High Street (*see* pp 33–4). The market cross was the secular focal point of the burgh. Burghs were established for trade, and Kirkcaldy's market was vital not only to the town itself, but also to the surrounding hinterland (*see* p 13). Because the geography and geology of the locality determined a distinctive layout for medieval settlement in Kirkcaldy (*see* pp 5–8), the town's market was inevitably a linear one. There was no open area, such as in, for example, Haddington and Inverkeithing, to house a 'market square'. Consequently, the other main elements of the market—the tolbooth and the tron (or weighing machine)—may have been placed further down the High Street. The old market cross, first referred to in 1590,[6] although it was probably much older, had fallen into disrepair by 1669. It was decided that the 'trie' or main shaft, which had collapsed, should be replaced and that the 'lion and unicorn' that topped it should be restored to their former position.[7] By 1734 the Council proposed to pull down the cross and replace it with a well, possibly feeding it with a lead pipe from the school well and the manse well.[8] This strongly suggests that the cross was, indeed, at the foot of Kirk Wynd, and not at the alternative site further west. Three years later a firm decision was made that 'as presently stands' the cross was 'of no manner

history

archaeology

chance finds

Port Brae NT 283 917 **F**
Perforated stone macehead Found at Port Brae and donated to Kirkcaldy Museum.

bore-hole surveys

Port Brae / High Street, 1982 **H**
Two separate surveys, carried out in 1992, revealed *c* 2–3 m of 'drift' deposits.

Adam Smith Close, south side **I**
A bore-hole survey carried out in advance of the 'Central Area Car Park' in 1981 revealed 'fills' ranging from 0.45 m to 2.35 m. These were mostly ash, but also revealed sandstone fragments, slag and gravel. The significant depth of these deposits and the high rubble

of use, but a nuisance'. The recommendation that the 'stones' should be rouped and 'put to the best advantage' suggests the cross was by now a more substantial stone structure.[9]

The tolbooth and the tron may also have been sited at the foot of Kirk Wynd **D**.[10] The tolbooth, along with the market cross, was the most important secular building, as it was here that market dues were collected and the town weights stored. It also functioned as the meeting place for the town council. Head courts, which were in theory attended by all burgesses, were also held in the tolbooth or on the common muir in summer months.[11] In 1566 a decision was made that the vault under the tolbooth should act as the town gaol.[12] Here were warded suspected witches, as well as felons, and although five people might be imprisoned at one time it was felt to be inadequate for Kirkcaldy's needs.[13] The records also indicate that repair work on the tolbooth was ongoing throughout the seventeenth century,[14] and in 1678, for both of these reasons, it was rebuilt. In the process a neighbouring small, thatched property was demolished without permission and the irate owner had to be compensated with 500 merks, even though the property was valued at only 300 merks.[15] By now, the tolbooth was sited at the top of the later-constructed Tolbooth Street **D**.[16] This structure was considerably larger than its predecessor, with at least three storeys. The ground floor housed a meal market, the public weigh house and the guard house, the first floor the council chambers, with, above, a gaol, with separate cells for debtors and criminals.[17] The construction of this new tolbooth, along with other building works, brought the town into debt. Parliament, therefore, deemed it appropriate in 1707 that the town should levy 2d on every pint of ale or beer brewed and sold in Kirkcaldy, over and above the excise tax, for a period of twenty-five years.[18] A new tolbooth, built in 1826, was demolished in 1935.

Running back from the High Street were the burgage plots, with dwellings on the

history frontages. In the backlands, most of which appear to have been undeveloped before the

archaeology element suggest that they represent the demolition of eighteenth- or early nineteenth-century buildings depicted on the Moore and Wood maps of 1809 and 1824 respectively **figure 19**.

future development

The Esplanade has been partially developed as a frontage, and further environmental improvements are proposed in the 1993 Local Plan, together with car parking at Tolbooth Street.

archaeological potential **figure 18**

This area, along with Area 5 **figure 15**, best reflects the medieval character of the town and, despite the limited opportunities so far presented, may offer the most archaeological potential. Previous excavations, supplemented by the bore-hole evidence, suggest two things: firstly, that the rubble derived from the demolition of the eighteenth- and nineteenth-century buildings in this area has largely been spread around and the ground level raised considerably; secondly, that pockets of medieval garden soils are still preserved within this area, sealed below the rubble. If areas of medieval garden soil survive, any structures that were situated within the backlands, such as out-buildings, rubbish pits and plot boundaries, may also survive. Archaeological monitoring of future development in this area would provide important evidence for its chronological development and some indication of the nature of its usage.

The archaeological potential of the High Street frontage in this area is unknown. A full study of the nature of cellarage on the High Street was beyond the scope of this survey, but nineteenth century, there was space for growing vegetables, keeping animals and housing wells, midden heaps and cesspits. On this side of the High Street the plots ran down to the shore, probably giving private beaching grounds to the burgesses resident here.

It is known that salt-pans were worked on the shore to the north of this area (*see* p 15 and **figure 19**). Panning may also have been a feature of the backlands.

Tolbooth Street was cut through the burgage plots in the eighteenth century to give access to the shore. Two standing houses on the north side of the street (*see* p 63) reveal the original style of building. The street is so named as the tolbooth once stood at the top, on the High Street.

notes

1	*KBR*, 99, 107.	11	MS Burgh Court Book (1.6.1), *passim*.
2	MS Burgh Court Book (1.6.3), 4 June 1593.	12	*KBR*, 68.
3	*Ibid*, 1 June 1601.	13	*RPC*, xii, 490; 2nd ser., vi, 396.
4	*Ibid*, 24 April 1605.	14	For example, MS Burgh Court Books (1.6.5), 8 October 1606; (1.6.6), 14 October 1607; (1.6.7), 12 October 1625.
5	*KBR*, 10.		
6	*KBR*, 135.		
7	*KBR*, 196.	15	*RPC*, viii, 518, 519, 617.
8	*KBR*, 261.	16	*OSA*, x, 507.
9	*KBR*, 262.	17	*OSA*, x, 507–8.
10	*KBR*, 10.	18	*APS*, xi, 482; *see also ibid*, x, 145.

history

archaeology

approximately half the street is thought to be cellared. There has been no previous work here, and as with all medieval High Streets or main thoroughfares, it must remain an archaeological priority.

Tolbooth Street appears to have been inserted in the eighteenth century, and the north side of the street immediately developed as a frontage. Traces of the earlier burgage plots, in the form of garden soils or even the plot boundaries themselves, may survive beneath the modern road surface.

The Esplanade, built in 1923 over an old trackway over the sands, now seals the eastern end of the High Street properties under 4–5 m of rubble. The west side of the Esplanade is increasingly being developed as a frontage, and monitoring of development here would allow the nature of the property boundaries at the end of the rigs to be assessed, with consideration given to the access they provided to the sea. The Esplanade itself is also of interest: salt-panning, an industry that dates back at least to the sixteenth century, is depicted on Wood's map of 1824 in this area **figure 19**. Although the salt-pans were clustered at the north end of the modern Esplanade, they could have extended further south. However, even with the proposed environmental improvements, the depth of made ground since dumped over this area renders any opportunity for a closer look at the earlier beach levels perhaps unlikely.

The discovery of the perforated stone macehead at Port Brae, although a chance find from an unknown context, demonstrates, as ever in Kirkcaldy, a potential for the survival of prehistoric remains—both from within the medieval core of the burgh and from the limits of the modern town. However, most of the material in this category has come from the area to the west of the High Street.

32

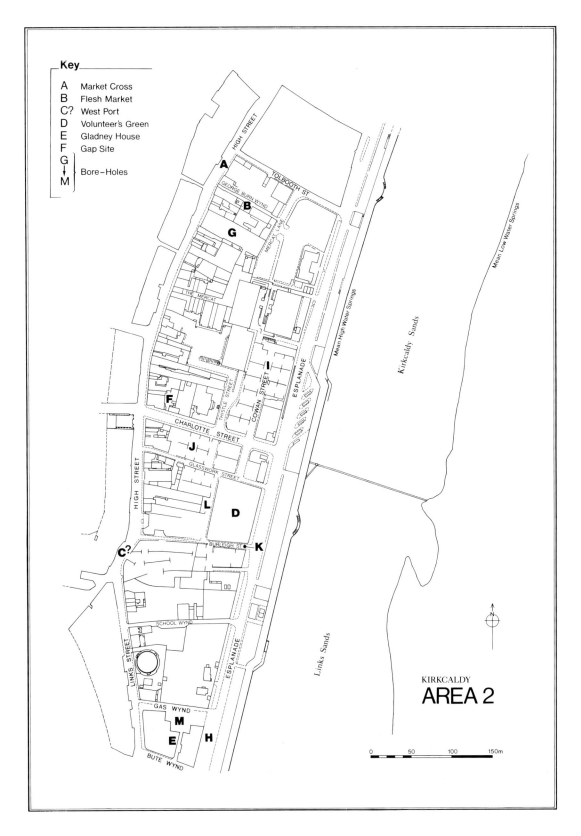

Key

A   Market Cross
B   Flesh Market
C?   West Port
D   Volunteer's Green
E   Gladney House
F   Gap Site
G
↓   Bore–Holes
M

KIRKCALDY
AREA 2

0   50   100   150m

figure 10

Area 2

area 2

Tolbooth Street to Charlotte Street / High Street / sea **figure 10**

description

This, the largest of the six arbitrary areas, is defined by the High Street to the west, the Esplanade to the east, Tolbooth Street to the north and Gas Wynd to the south. There is little value in sub-dividing this area, with almost half of it encapsulated within a sprawling, city centre development, comprising a shopping mall (1981–3), multi-storey car parks (1981–3) and a swimming pool (*c* 1970). As a result, Rose Street, which is depicted on Moore's map, has now completely disappeared.

Much of the central area is already laid out as long-term, landscaped, terraced parking. In recent years Thistle Street has been extended southwards, cutting across Charlotte Street, and past Volunteers' Green, before joining up with Burleigh Street. Burleigh Street itself appears to have been substantially widened, particularly around the High Street/ Nicol Street and Esplanade junctions.

Volunteers' Green **D** appears to have been an open area from at least the time of Moore's 1809 map of the town, the name suggesting that it was used as a training ground for the local militia. It is now a walled garden area, with some modern landscaping and ornamental features.

The south end has also been redeveloped recently, with large, 'out of town' style retail units, and associated customer car parking to the north and south of Louden's Wynd. The extreme south end of this area, however, still retains some character. Here, the narrow vennels of Louden's Wynd (the old border between Kirkcaldy and Linktown), School Wynd, Gas Wynd and Hendry's Wynd connect the High Street with the Esplanade and provide relief from a rather depressing modern townscape.

The area around Gas Wynd is largely open ground, with some modern offices and associated car parking. This was the site of the old gas works and still appears to belong to British Gas.

One of the few gap sites in this block with development potential **F** is at the western end of Charlotte Street (north side) and is currently being used as a temporary public car park (7 Charlotte Street).

historical background

At the north end of this area, in the middle of the High Street, marked by a cross on the ground **A**, is one of the two possible sites of the old market cross (*see* p 29). The market cross was the secular focal point of the burgh. Burghs were established for trade, and Kirkcaldy's market was vital not only to the town itself, but also to the surrounding

previous archaeological work

To date there has been no archaeological work carried out, modern or antiquarian, within this area.

chance finds

No chance finds have been reported from this area.

bore-hole surveys

134–144 High Street **G**

Bore-holes carried out in advance of a BHS development in 1963 revealed mostly sand

34

hinterland (*see* p 13). Because the geography and geology of the locality determined a distinctive layout for medieval settlement in Kirkcaldy (*see* pp 5–7), the town's market was a linear one. There was no open area, such as in, for example, Haddington and Inverkeithing, to house a 'market square'. Consequently, the other main elements of the market—the tolbooth and the tron (or weighing machine)—may have been placed further up the High Street (*see* pp 29–30). The old market cross, first referred to in 1590,[1] although it was probably much older, had fallen into disrepair by 1669. It was decided that the 'trie' or main shaft, which had collapsed, should be replaced and that the 'lion and unicorn' that topped it should be restored to their former position.[2] By 1734 the council proposed to pull down the cross and replace it with a well, possibly feeding it with a lead pipe from the school well and the manse well.[3] This strongly suggests that the cross was, indeed, at the foot of Kirk Wynd, and not at this site marked on the ground. Three years later a firm decision was made that 'as presently stands' the cross was 'of no manner of use, but a nuisance'. The recommendation that the 'stones' should be rouped and 'put to the best advantage' suggests that the cross was by now a more substantial stone structure.[4]

Running back from the High Street were the burgage plots, with dwellings on the frontages. In the backlands, most of which appear to have been undeveloped before the nineteenth century, there was space for growing vegetables, keeping animals and housing wells, midden heaps and cesspits. On this side of the High Street the plots ran down to the shore, probably giving private beaching grounds to the burgesses resident here.

It is known that salt-pans were worked on the shore to the north of this area (*see* p 15 and **figure 19**). Panning may also have been a feature of the backlands.

A few of the standing properties fronting the High Street reveal the prosperity of Kirkcaldy in the earlier part of the nineteenth century (*see* pp 63–4). Nos 148, 152 and 156 are worthy of note. The child poetess, Marjorie Fleming, was born in no 132. No 162 is on

history

---

archaeology

and gravel at ground level. However, 3 ft (1 m) of topsoil was found in two of them and cobbles in a third.

Esplanade, Hendry's Wynd to Port Brae **H**
A bore-hole survey along the Esplanade revealed between 0.6 and 4.80 m of 'fill', comprising rubble, top soil, clay, ash, cinders and gravel. The presence of crockery in these deposits suggests some levelling prior to the construction of the Esplanade in 1923. The crockery may have come from some of the many potteries established in Kirkcaldy by the late nineteenth century: the four largest were the Kirkcaldy Pottery in Linktown, and the Fife Pottery, Morrison & Crawford's and the Sinclairtown Pottery, all in the Gallatown. *The Excavations at Sinclairtown Pottery, Kirkcaldy* (Fife Regional Council, Glenrothes, 1991).

Esplanade / Cowan Street **I**
In advance of construction of the multi-storey car park in 1980 a series of bore-holes were recorded. Up to 1.8 m of 'fill' was observed, comprising old brick/rubble foundations.

Charlotte Street / Glasswork Street **J**
A bore-hole survey was carried out in advance of construction of a car park in 1980. Between 0.25 and 0.75 m of 'fill' was recorded.

Burleigh Street **K**
During a bore-hole survey in 1980 at the east end of Burleigh Street, up to 1.68 m of rubble, ash, sand and gravel was recorded.

Thistle Street **L**
Between 0.45 and 1 m of predominantly dark sand, sandstone, ash and gravel was recorded during a bore-hole survey.

the site of the old fleshmarket **B**, beside one of Kirkcaldy's burns, the Balcanquhal Burn, named after George Balcanquhal, bailie, and remembered in the name 'George Burn Wynd' **C**. The fleshmarket was temporarily removed from the George Burn and in 1669 the fleshers requested its return to the former site. Slaughtering and butchering in the central area of the town were not, however, ideal, and the council decided to remove the fleshmarket to the West Port, a less populated area.[5]

This location was adequately maintained by the council, a ruling being made that paving should be laid outside the West Port as far as Richard Boswell's Wynd as early as 1608 (although the order may not have been immediately obeyed).[6] Two years earlier, Richard Boswell and one other were instructed to repair the dyke fronting the common vennel; Boswell was to clear the West Burn of a tree growing out of his yard and fouling the burn.[7]

At the southern end of this area is the site of the West Port **C**. Its exact location on the High Street is not known, but it was around present-day Burleigh Street/Nicol Wynd. Tradition suggests that it was at Louden's Wynd, the burgh boundary being at the channel of a prehistoric river. Ports, or gates, usually simple wooden barresses, were common features in medieval burghs. This port was, apparently, in a ruinous state by 1674. It was to be rebuilt, or at least repaired, in 'caslor work', which implies a more substantial structure.[8] Ports' primary function was to monitor access to the burgh. In particular they controlled entrance to the burgh market, the use of which demanded the payment of a toll, or tax, at the port or at the tolbooth (*see* pp 29–30), and excluded potential carriers of plague during outbreaks of the 'pestilence' or 'pest'. In 1585, during a plague scare, it was decided that, apart from parishioners who were permitted to enter the burgh at the Kirk Wynd Port, all strangers were to be denied access by the West Port and were to approach the town by the East Port for scrutiny.[9] Ports were usually set in walls surrounding the

Gas Wynd **M**

Between 0.20 and 1.10 m of 'fill' was recorded during a bore-hole survey, in advance of a housing development. Shallow coal workings were also identified below the site.

future development

The only development proposed in the Finalised Local Plan for this area, which also affects Area 1, involves environmental improvements along the Esplanade.

archaeological potential **figure 18**

In view of the scale of development in recent years in this area and the disappearance of identifiable older properties extending from the High Street eastwards, it would seem unlikely that archaeological deposits survive to any great extent within Area 2, except the High Street frontage itself. Archaeological potential must therefore be seen as low. However, this assessment should be viewed as provisional, given the lack of previous archaeological work and chance finds.

The potential of the High Street frontage, perhaps the only archaeological opportunity remaining in this area, is also largely unknown. However, the bore-hole evidence from **G** indicated that up to 1 m of stratigraphy and possible structural remains survived prior to development. Therefore, positive evidence of preservation on the frontage exists and, as with all medieval High Streets or main thoroughfares, it must remain an archaeological priority.

Monitoring of development here may offer the opportunity to answer a range of archaeological questions concerning this area, not only about the nature of the structures on the frontage but also about the chronology of the development of this part of the burgh. More specifically, the nature of usage of the backlands—and their contrast with those on the westward side of the High Street—needs to be assessed.

36

town, but most Scottish burghs, Kirkcaldy included, did not have stone encircling walls, relying for a measure of security on small, probably wooden, fences at the end of burgage plots. In all probability, although to date there is no evidence, a simple dyke passed from the shore to the West Port, and from there to the rear of the burgage plots to the west of High Street. There is no evidence, archaeological or documentary, of ditching, as is found in some burghs.

The West Port gave access to the burgh muirs and common lands, the buttis, the Tiel Burn, the West Bridge and West Mill, and St Catherine's Chapel, as well as to the independent burgh of barony, Linktown. Volunteers' Green, **D** the vestiges of which can be seen beside the Presto car park, was exchanged by the town council in the 1880s for an alternative plot of land some small distance to the south-west. This alternative plot of land was all that remained of the town's common muir and pasturings, later used for bleaching and drying linen, and for recreation. Outwith the town port, in Bute Street, Linktown, stood Gladney House, the home of Robert and James Adam, architects **E**. A fine example of Scottish classical architecture and built in 1711, it was allowed to decline into a dilapidated state and demolished in 1931.

notes

1	*KBR*, 135.		6	MS Court Book (1.6.6), 12 October 1608.
2	*KBR*, 196.			
3	*KBR*, 261.		7	MS Court Book (1.6.5), 8 October 1606.
4	*KBR*, 262.			
history	5	*KBR*, 195.	8	*KBR*, 204.
			9	*KBR*, 99, 107.

archaeology

A full study of the nature of cellarage on the High Street would be a worthwhile undertaking for the future, and would help to inform this assessment. Approximately half is thought to be cellared.

The Esplanade, built in 1923 over an old trackway over the sands, now seals the eastern end of the High Street properties under 4–5 m of rubble and, unfortunately, obscures the important relationship between the end of the plots and the sea-shore.

Perhaps of interest to industrial archaeologists or historians, bore-hole evidence from the south end of this block **M** revealed shallow coal workings of unknown date, approximately 20 m below the ground surface. Another working was identified immediately to the west of Links Street (*see* Area 3).

area 3

Nicol Street to Balfour Place / Bell Inn Wynd / High Street / Douglas Street / Whytehouse Avenue / Hunter Place / Hunter Street **figure 11**

description

This area is defined by the High Sreet to the east, Balfour Place and Bell Inn Wynd to the north, and the junction of Nicol Street and High Street to the south. The western boundary is physically less well defined, but comprises Douglas Street, Whytehouse Avenue, Park Place, Hunter Place and Hunter Street.

The junction between High Street, Nicol Street and Burleigh Street has been substantially widened in recent years, and marks the southern end of this area. From this point the High Street continues southwards, but named as Links Street.

Immediately to the north of this junction lies the old indoor market, the Olympia Arcade **J**, still partly in use but generally run down. The houses that front westwards onto Douglas Street have open gardens that extend down towards, and close to, the High Street. The gardens of these properties display a remarkable regularity, suggesting that they are a more recent feature, rather than fossilised medieval burgage plots.

The gardens here look down on a narrow strip of development forming the west frontage of the High Street, and highlight a feature which is constant throughout all three areas to the west of the High Street (Areas 3, 4 and 5): the significant slope up from the High Street and the degree of terracing which has taken place to accommodate it **figures 3 & 6**.

In the central area, defined by Whytehouse Avenue, Park Place, Whytescauseway and High Street, there is a largely open space, surrounding the Carlton Bakery **H**. Backing onto this, from the south-west, are a number of private gardens attached to the houses fronting onto Whytescauseway. An irregular passage **I** cuts through this area, connecting Whytescauseway with Whytehouse Avenue, appearing almost as a southern extension of Hill Street.

A large tract of the northern section of this area is taken up by the bus station, with most of the area between Hill Street and Hunter Street being encapsulated within a large, modern shopping complex (The Postings). Some small open areas still survive, to the rear of the properties that front onto the High Street, between Lady Inn Wynd and Bell Inn Wynd. Again, these small, narrow wynds break the monotony of the modern landscape and add some colour.

historical background

At the southern end of this area is the site of the West Port **A**. Its exact location on the High Street is not known, but it was around present-day Burleigh Street / Nicol Wynd; tradition suggests that it was at Louden's Wynd, the burgh boundary being at the channel of a prehistoric river. Ports, or gates, usually simple wooden barresses, were common features in medieval burghs. This port was, apparently, in a ruinous state by 1674. It was

history

archaeology

previous archaeological work

113 High Street NT *280 914* **B**

A watching brief was carried out in April 1993 on the insertion of a new pipe trench to the rear of the property at 113 High Street. The trench, aligned north to south towards Hill Street, was cut to a depth of 0.75 m. A thick, brown clay deposit, possibly natural, was observed *c* 0.58 m below the modern ground surface. Sealing the natural was a 0.40 m thick sandy clay layer, possibly a garden soil, with frequent charcoal and stone inclusions.

38

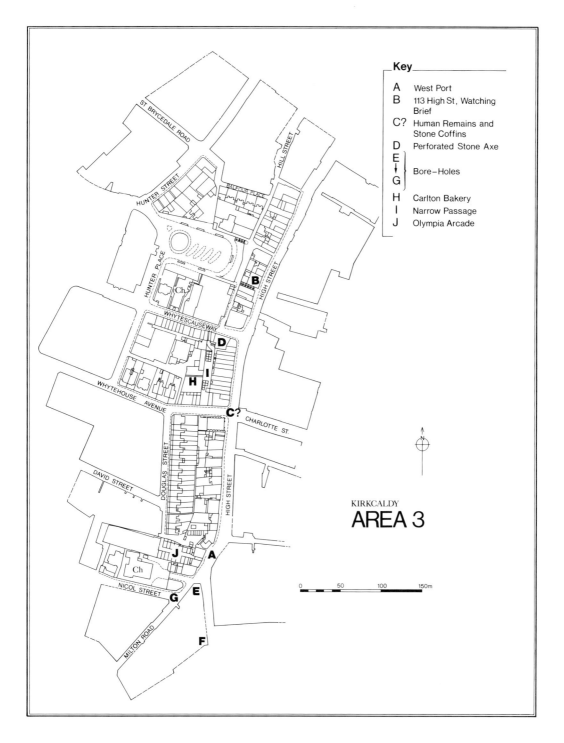

Key

A   West Port
B   113 High St, Watching Brief
C?   Human Remains and Stone Coffins
D   Perforated Stone Axe
E
↓   Bore-Holes
G
H   Carlton Bakery
I   Narrow Passage
J   Olympia Arcade

KIRKCALDY
AREA 3

0   50   100   150m

figure 11

Area 3

to be rebuilt, or at least repaired, in 'caslor work', which implies a more substantial structure.[1] Ports' primary function was to monitor access to the burgh. In particular this involved controlling entrance to the burgh market, the use of which demanded the payment of a toll, or tax, at the port or at the tolbooth (*see* pp 29–30), and excluding potential carriers of plague during outbreaks of the 'pestilence' or 'pest'. In 1585, during a plague scare, it was decided that, apart from parishioners who were permitted to enter the burgh at the Kirk Wynd Port, all strangers were to be denied access by the West Port and were to approach the town by the East Port for scrutiny.[2] The port gave access to the burgh muirs and common lands, the buttis, the Tiel Burn, the West Bridge and West Mill, and St Catherine's Chapel, as well as to the independent burgh of barony, Linktown. Ports were usually set in walls surrounding the town but most Scottish burghs, Kirkcaldy included, did not have stone encircling walls, relying for a measure of security on small, probably wooden, fences at the end of burgage plots. In all probability, although to date there is no evidence, a simple dyke passed from the shore to the West Port, and from there to the rear of the burgage plots to the west of High Street. There is no evidence, archaeological or documentary, of ditching, as is found in some burghs.

From 1669 the fleshmarket was at the West Port, having been moved from a more central location. Slaughtering and butchering in the central area of the town were not, however, ideal, and the council decided to remove the fleshmarket to a less populated area.[3]

This location, however, was adequately maintained by the council, a ruling being made that paving should be laid outside the West Port as far as Richard Boswell's Wynd as early

history

---

archaeology

This produced a single sherd of late medieval pottery. A series of flagstones, set into a bedding layer, above the garden soil, may have formed a yard surface, of Victorian or later date. SUAT Archive Report (1993, unpublished).

chance finds

High Street NT 2791 9101–2832 9177 **C**
Stone coffins, human remains, sculptured arms and inscriptions were discovered in different places by workmen digging foundations in the nineteenth century. They furnish grounds for supposing that a religious house must at one time have stood on the west side of the High Street. *NSA*, ix, 748.

Whytehouse Mansions NT 279 912 **D**
Perforated stone axe.
Donated to Kirkcaldy Museum.

bore-hole surveys

Milton Road **E**
A bore-hole survey was carried out in 1991, in advance of construction of a car park. Between 0.20 m and 1.20 m of 'fill', containing some ash, was recorded.

Link St **F**
In advance of the construction of Kingdom Hall and a housing development, a bore-hole survey was carried out. A worked coal seam, at a shallow depth (20 m), was identified beneath the site. Between 0.20 and 0.90 m of 'fill', including clay and ash, was recorded as overlying the natural sub-soil.

Nicol Street **G**
'Fills', ranging from 0.20 to 4.75 m were recorded in advance of road widening and a car park in 1982.

40

as 1608 (although the order may not have been immediately obeyed).[4] Two years earlier Richard Boswell and one other were instructed to repair the dyke fronting the common vennel; Boswell was to clear the West Burn of a tree growing out of his yard and fouling the burn.[5]

Running back from the High Street were the burgage plots, with dwellings on the frontages. In the backlands, most of which appear to have been undeveloped before the early nineteenth century, there was space for growing vegetables, keeping animals and housing wells, midden heaps and cesspits. On this side of the High Street the medieval plots terminated at the cliff-like edge of the raised beach (*see* pp 5–6), although terracing reduced the sharpness of the slope **figures 3** & **6**. The encircling fencing at the rear of the plots had small gates leading from the burgage plots to the countryside. Cartographic evidence suggests that development up the hill, beyond the traditional burgh confines, had commenced by the later nineteenth century.

A number of the standing properties on the frontages (*see* pp 63–4) reveal the wealth of Kirkcaldy during the earlier part of the nineteenth century. Nos 125, 133–35, and 151 are particularly worth noting.

notes

1	*KBR*, 204.	4	MS Court Book (1.6.6), 12 October 1608.
2	*KBR*, 177, 99, 107.		
history 3	*KBR*, 195.	5	MS Court Book (1.6.5), 8 October 1606.

archaeology

future development

No development is proposed in the finalised Local Plan for this area.

archaeological potential **figure 18**

A study of the topography, or physical setting, of the burgh for this survey (*see* pp 5–7) has suggested that the westward development of the medieval burgh was constricted by the slope that rises westwards from the High Street—a rise of *c* 7 m over a distance of less than 150 m. It would seem that the medieval settlement in this part of the town (*see also* Areas 4 and 5) comprised a narrow strip along the west of the High Street. This interpretation would seem to be confirmed by Moore's map of 1809, which shows the burgage plots in this area as being considerably smaller than those to the east of the High Street.

A narrow back lane originally ran behind the burgage plots to the west of the High Street, from Kirk Wynd, southwards. This would eventually become developed as Hill Street. The land to the west of Hill Street was settled, perhaps as a secondary phase of development.

The implications of development on the potential archaeology of this area are therefore centred around the narrow strip along the western frontage of the High Street. The actual potential of the High Street frontage in this area is unknown. However, the discovery in the nineteenth century of stone coffins and human remains at various locations on the west side of the High Street, coupled with the survival of medieval garden soils to the rear of 113 High Street, suggest that survival of archaeological deposits is highly probable here. A full study of the nature of cellarage on the High Street was beyond the scope of this survey, but approximately half is thought to be cellared.

The discovery of sculptured arms and inscriptions with the stone coffins and human remains implies that these are probably late in date. However, without an accurate location or description of the finds, little more can be said concerning the possible existence of a religious house on the west side of the High Street.

Monitoring of development here may offer the opportunity to answer a range of archaeology

archaeological questions, not only about the nature of the structures on the frontage but also about the chronology of the development of this part of the burgh. More specifically, the nature of usage of the backlands, and how they compared with those on the seaward side of the High Street, needs to be assessed. Finally, the nature of the property boundaries at the end of the rigs that marked the western limit of the burgh should also be assessed.

The scale of recent development, particularly at the northern end of this area, and the degree of terracing to the west of this narrow strip, suggest that the rest of the area has a low archaeological potential. Cartographic evidence also indicates that much of this area was still open ground, even in the early nineteenth century, and part of large private estates **figure 19**.

The bore-hole evidence has also demonstrated little potential for the preservation of archaeological deposits in the areas surveyed. It has, however, identified shallow coal workings, some 20 m below the ground surface, to the west of Links Street, which will be of interest to industrial archaeologists and historians.

The discovery of a polished stone axe at Whytehouse Mansions is a clear indicator of the potential for prehistoric archaeological remains on the west side of the High Street. A number of cist burials in the vicinity (*see* p 44), again concentrated on the western side of the High Street, are also testament to the attractiveness of the Kirkcaldy area in prehistory.

42

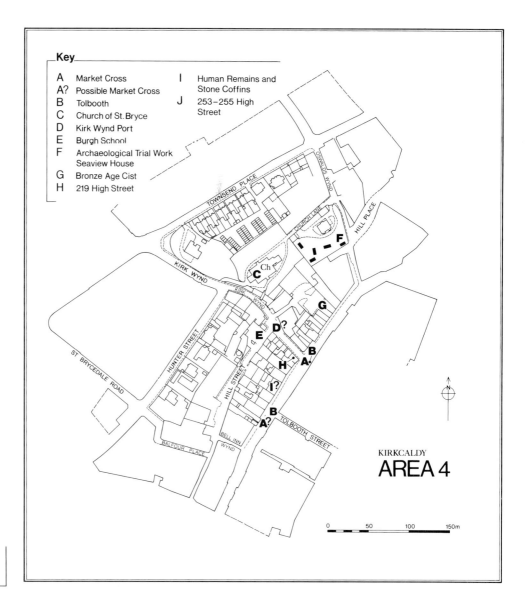

Key

A   Market Cross
A? Possible Market Cross
B   Tolbooth
C   Church of St. Bryce
D   Kirk Wynd Port
E   Burgh School
F   Archaeological Trial Work
     Seaview House
G   Bronze Age Cist
H   219 High Street

I   Human Remains and
    Stone Coffins
J   253–255 High
    Street

KIRKCALDY
AREA 4

figure 12

Area 4

figure 13

Lintel, 225–229 High
Street, demolished
© *Crown Copyright:*
RCAHMS

area 4

Balfour Place/Bell Inn Wynd/High Street/Oswald's Wynd/Townsend Place/Hunter Street
figure 12

description

This block is defined by Balfour Place and Bell Inn Wynd to the south, High Street to the east, Hunter Street and Townsend Place to the west, and Oswald's Wynd to the north, and incorporates Kirk Wynd.

With Kirk Wynd dividing this area in two, it can be further sub-divided into two smaller units, the first to the south of Kirk Wynd and the second to the north. Most of the southern section of this area, up to Kirk Wynd, has been recently developed as a shopping centre (The Postings), together with some new housing along the the east side of Hunter Street.

To the east of Hill Street, there are some small parcels of open ground to the rear of, and associated with, the buildings fronting onto the High Street, mostly in use as staff and customer parking.

There is one significant vacant property on the High Street frontage. At the junction with Kirk Wynd, 219 High Street (*see* p 63), dating to the eighteenth century, has fallen into what may be a terminal state of disrepair **H**.

The northern section of this area contains some of the few areas of open, possibly undeveloped, ground left within or near the core of the medieval burgh. Much of the area around the parish church is still open, comprising the grounds of both the manse to the west and Seaview House to the north, as is some ground associated with properties 243–255 High Street **J**.

Private residential housing fronts on to Townsend Place, with garages and parking to the rear backing onto the kirkyard cemetery. Church Lane provides a popular short cut from Oswald's Wynd (Dishington's Wynd on Moore's map of 1809), through the kirkyard, to Kirk Wynd. A large, now redundant factory, to the west of Church Lane, occupies much of the rest of this block.

historic background

This area was the hub of medieval Kirkcaldy. Running back from the High Street were the burgage plots, with dwellings on the frontages. In the backlands, most of which appear to have been undeveloped before the nineteenth century, there was space for growing vegetables, keeping animals and housing wells, midden heaps and cesspits. Some prestigious dwellings were sited here by the late eighteenth and early nineteenth centuries. Photographs of the now demolished 225–229 High Street indicate the quality of building that once stood in this area **figure 13**.

On this side of the High Street the medieval plots terminated at the cliff-like edge of the raised beach (*see* pp 5–6), although terracing reduced the sharpness of the slope. The

previous archaeological work

Seaview House, Oswald's Wynd/Church Lane NT 2815 9173 **F**

An assessment was carried out, in June 1994, in the walled garden of a nineteenth-century house, where it was proposed to construct a block of thirty-two flats and associated car parking facilities. The archaeological potential was considered to be good as this area appeared from cartographic sources to have been an open garden since at least 1809. It was thought possible that the parish church graveyard to the south of the site might originally have extended beyond its present boundary. A series of at least three well-defined encircling fencing at the rear of the plots had small gates leading from the burgage plots to, in some cases, a back lane and then to the countryside. Cartographic evidence suggests that development up the hill, beyond the traditional burgh confines, had commenced by the later nineteenth century.

In the middle ages this area would have been one of the most desirable, being close to the market. The market cross was the secular focal point of the burgh. There are two possible sites for the cross: at the foot of Kirk Wynd and in the middle of the High Street opposite the modern Marks and Spencers **A**.[1] Burghs were established for trade, and Kirkcaldy's market was vital not only to the town itself, but also to the surrounding hinterland (*see* p 13). Because the geography and geology of the locality determined a distinctive layout for medieval settlement in Kirkcaldy (*see* pp 5–6), the town's market was a linear one. There was no open area, such as in, for example, Haddington and Inverkeithing, to house a 'market square'. Consequently, the other main elements of the market—the tolbooth and the tron (or weighing machine)—may have been placed further down the High Street **B**. The old market cross, first referred to in 1590,[2] although it was probably much older, had fallen into disrepair by 1669. It was decided that the 'trie' or main shaft, which had collapsed, should be replaced and that the 'lion and unicorn' that topped it should be restored to their former position.[3] By 1734 the council proposed to pull down the cross and replace it with a well, possibly feeding it with a lead pipe from the school well and the manse well.[4] Such a consideration strongly suggests that the cross was, indeed, at the foot of Kirk Wynd, and not at the alternative suggested site further west. Three years later, a firm decision was made that 'as presently stands' the cross was 'of no manner of use, but a nuisance'. The recommendation that the 'stones' should be rouped and 'put to the best advantage' suggests that the cross was by now a more substantial stone

history

structure.[5]

---

archaeology

terraces could be seen, cut into the slope of the hill. Five trenches were opened by mechanical excavator across the site.

The trenches revealed an accumulation of primarily eighteenth- and nineteenth-century garden soils, ranging in depth from 1 m at the west end to over 2 m at the east end. The terraces were of the same date, and traces of possible ornamental garden features were identified. Furrows in the natural sand in one of the trenches, sealed by a layer containing a seventeenth-century clay pipe, may indicate late medieval cultivation. Only one sherd of late fifteenth- or sixteenth-century pottery, from a possible pit or gully, was recovered. SUAT Archive Report (1994, unpublished).

High Street NT 281 916 **G**
Demolition and foundation clearance revealed the remains of three cists. One cist, set in pure sand, was almost completely destroyed; the others were partly preserved in recent cement and house foundations. Two cists contained inhumed remains, which showed traces of burning. One of these burials had a food vessel, flint arrowhead and flint knife in association. *DES* (1980), 5.

chance finds

High Street NT 2791 91012832 9177 **I**
Stone coffins, human remains, sculptured arms and inscriptions were discovered in different places by workmen digging foundations in the nineteenth century. They furnish grounds for supposing that a religious house must at one time have stood on the west side of the High Street. *NSA*, ix, 748.

bore-hole surveys

No bore-hole surveys have been carried out within this area.

The tolbooth **B** and the tron may also have been sited at the foot of Kirk Wynd.[6] The tolbooth, along with the market cross, was the most important secular building, as it was here that market dues were collected and the town weights stored. It also functioned as the meeting place for the town council. Head courts, which were in theory attended by all burgesses, were held in the tolbooth or on the common muir in summer months.[7] In 1566 a decision was made that the vault under the tolbooth should act as the town gaol.[8] Here were warded suspected witches, as well as felons, and although five people might be imprisoned at one time it was felt to be inadequate for Kirkcaldy's needs.[9] The records also indicate that repair work on the tolbooth was ongoing throughout the seventeenth century,[10] and in 1678, for both of these reasons, it was rebuilt. In the process a neighbouring small, thatched property was demolished without permission and the irate owner had to be compensated with 500 merks, even though the property was valued at only 300 merks.[11] By now, the tolbooth was sited at the top of the later Tolbooth Street **D**.[12] This structure was considerably larger than its predecessor, with a minimum of three storeys. The ground floor housed a meal market, the public weigh house and the guard house, the first floor the council chambers, with, above, a jail, with separate cells for debtors and criminals.[13] The construction of this new tolbooth, along with other building works, brought the town into debt. Parliament, therefore, deemed it appropriate that the town should levy 2d on every pint of ale or beer brewed and sold in Kirkcaldy, over and above the excise tax, for a period of twenty-five years.[14] A new town house, built in 1826, was demolished in 1935.

Kirk Wynd, as the name suggests, led to the burgh church of St Bryce **C** **figure 14**. When this site was first occupied by a religious establishment is uncertain; but Kirkcaldy shire had a church at least by a date between 1124 and 1131, when David I granted the shire of Kirkcaldy and its church to Dunfermline Abbey.[15] By 1182 there is specific

figure 14
Kirk Wynd
*Kirkcaldy
Museum and Art
Gallery*

mention of the 'town and church of Kirkcaldy' ('villam et ecclesiam de Kircaldin') and in 1194 of 'all Kirkcaldy with the church' ('totam Kircaldii cum ecclesia'), both of which strongly suggest a church connected with the town.[16] Whether this church was on the small hill to the west of the town is unclear, but it does seem that the church gifted by David de Bernham, bishop of St Andrews, to the abbey of Dunfermline in 1240, and dedicated by him to St Patrick and St Bryce in 1244, was on this site.[17] Little is known of its medieval past, other than that a number of altars were supported within the church: the Holy Rood altar,[18] the altar of St Anne,[19] and the Holy Blood altar are mentioned.[20] Once the burgh records are extant, it can be seen that the town council was maintaining the fabric of the church, under the care of annually appointed kirkmasters.[21]

The building was often in disrepair. Constant efforts were made in the later sixteenth century to mend window glass, patch roofing and rebuild the kirkyard dykes.[22] A decision was also made to extend the burial ground beside the church, and to that end the church dyke was extended outwards.[23] The church seems to have accommodated a growing number of parishioners during the seventeenth century: a second minister was appointed in 1612 and the building was enlarged with a longer and wider north aisle in 1644. The church also prospered financially, and in 1706 it was able to lend 600 merks to the impoverished town council.[24] The fabric of the church deteriorated in the eighteenth century and a decision was made to rebuild it in 1807, money being partially raised by the sale of the poorhouse next door. The work was badly carried out and in June 1828 the north gallery of the church collapsed, leaving twenty-eight people dead and a hundred and fifty injured. Many improvements have been made since that time, leaving only the

history   west tower of the church as a medieval remnant.

archaeology

future development

No future development was proposed within the finalised Local Plan for this area.

archaeological potential **figure 18**

The northern section of this area has escaped much of the redevelopment of the town, and with such a high proportion of open ground, it has good archaeological potential. However, this must be balanced against the disappointing results of recent archaeological work at Seaview House, which suggest that this western area appears also to have been largely open ground in the medieval period. The lack of medieval pottery, for instance, is significant for an area close to the High Street; it suggests that the backlands of the properties fronting onto the High Street, and therefore the medieval burgh itself, did not extend this far west. This would imply that the parish church originally stood in isolation, overlooking the burgh. The absence of burials also suggests that the medieval boundaries of the kirkyard to the parish church have remained unchanged.

A study of the topography, or physical setting, of the burgh for this survey (*see* pp 5–7) has suggested that the westward development of the medieval burgh was constricted by the slope that rises westwards from the High Street—a rise of *c* 7 m over a distance of less than 150 m. Therefore it would seem that the medieval settlement in this part of the town (*see also* Areas 3 and 5) comprised a narrow strip along the west of the High Street **figure 3**. This interpretation would seem to be confirmed by Moore's map of 1809, which shows the burgage plots in this area as being smaller than those to the east of the High Street.

A narrow back lane originally ran behind the burgage plots to the west of the High Street, from Kirk Wynd, southwards. This would eventually become developed as Hill Street. The land to the west of Hill Street was settled, perhaps as a secondary phase of development.

Although documentary evidence does not specify it, archaeological research suggests that the church may have stood outwith the technical burgh boundaries, beyond one of the town's three ports, the Kirk Wynd Port **D**. Ports, or gates, usually simple wooden barresses, were common features in medieval burghs. Their primary function was to monitor access to the burgh. In particular they controlled entrance to the burgh market, the use of which demanded the payment of a toll, or tax, at the port or at the tolbooth (*see* p 30), and excluded potential carriers of plague during outbreaks of the 'pestilence' or 'pest'. In 1585, during a plague scare, it was decided that, apart from parishioners who were permitted to enter the burgh at the Kirk Wynd Port, all 'strangers' were to be denied access by the West Port and were to approach the town by the East Port for scrutiny.[25] Ports were usually set in walls surrounding the town but most Scottish burghs, Kirkcaldy included, did not have stone encircling walls, relying for a measure of security on small, probably wooden, fences at the end of burgage plots. There is no evidence, archaeological or documentary, of ditching, as is found in some burghs.

Two houses of interest stand on Kirk Wynd, giving solitary clues to the seventeenth- and early eighteenth-century architecture of the town (*see* p 63). Andersoune's House, beside the church, is in a good state of repair, although somewhat altered. The house on the west corner of Kirk Wynd and High Street has been allowed to deteriorate, in spite of its historical importance to the town **figure 14**. In July 1994 permission to demolish was given by Kirkcaldy District Council.

At the junction of Hill Street and Kirk Wynd stood the old burgh school (1725–1843) **E**, where Thomas Carlyle taught from 1816 to 1818. His house stood at 22 Kirk Wynd. Both buildings are demolished. Both Adam Smith and Robert Adam attended this school,

history

archaeology

The implications of development on the archaeological potential of this area are therefore centred around the narrow strip along the western frontage of the High Street, both frontages of Kirk Wynd and the area around the old parish church. The archaeological potential of these frontages is largely unknown. However, the discovery in the nineteenth century of stone coffins and human remains at various locations on the west side of the High Street, coupled with the survival of Bronze Age cist burials to the rear of 215–217 High Street, suggest that survival of archaeological deposits is highly probable, on or near the frontage. Although the results from Seaview House suggest that the western part of this block was open ground, and perhaps not backlands, the vacant ground to the rear of 243–255 High Street should offer more archaeological potential.

A full study of the nature of cellarage on the High Street was beyond the scope of this survey, but approximately half is thought to be cellared.

Monitoring of development here may offer the opportunity to answer a range of archaeological questions concerning this area, not only about the nature of the structures on the frontage, but also about the chronology of the development of this part of the burgh. More specifically, the nature of usage of the backlands, and their contrast with those on the seaward side of the High Street, needs to be assessed. Also, the nature of the property boundaries at the end of the rigs that marked the western limit of the burgh should be assessed. Finally, the parish church, perhaps standing in isolation overlooking the burgh, must also be considered (*see* pp 16, 61).

The discovery of the sculptured arms and inscriptions with the stone coffins and human remains implies that these are probably late in date. However, without an accurate location or description of the finds, little more can be said concerning the possible existence of a religious house on the west side of the High Street.

The discovery of three cist burials within this area is a clear indicator of the potential for prehistoric archaeological remains on the west side of the High Street, and a testament to the attractiveness of the Kirkcaldy area in prehistory.

48

the former from 1729 to 1737 and the latter from 1734 to 1739. Kirkcaldy had previously had the services of both a song school and a grammar school; Mr David Spens, the minister, was contracted to teach a grammar school in 1582, which would be supported by the entrance of some pupils from the existing song school. There being no school building, they were to be taught in the minister's house until alternative arrangements were made. In 1587 the council decreed that the building of a schoolhouse was to be 'set forward', but whether this was done is not clear.[26] The presbytery records in 1636, however, do refer to a school.[27]

North of Kirk Wynd runs Oswald's Wynd **H**. Once called Dishington's Wynd, sometime after 1820 it was renamed Oswald's Wynd after Sir John Oswald. He had built a town house here, in the late seventeenth century, Old Dunnikier House **figure 16**, in order to meet the residential qualification for members of the town council, residents of Pathhead being debarred from such honour in Kirkcaldy.

notes

1   *KBR*, 10.
2   *KBR*, 135.
3   *KBR*, 196.
4   *KBR*, 261.
5   *KBR*, 262.
6   *KBR*, 10.
7   MS Burgh Court Book (1.6.1), *passim*.
8   *KBR*, 68.
9   *RPC*, xii, 490; 2nd ser, vi, 396.
10   For example, MS Burgh Court Books (1.6.5), 8 October 1606; (1.6.6), 14 October 1607; (1.6.7), 12 October 1625.
11   *RPC*, viii, 518, 519, 617.
12   *OSA*, x, 507.
13   *OSA*, x, 507–8.
14   *APS*, ix, 482.
15   *Dunf Reg*, no 29.
16   *Ibid*, nos 238, 239.
17   J Irvine, *Kirkcaldy Old Parish Church*, 1244–1944 (Kirkcaldy, 1994), 2.

18   *Dunf Reg*, no 517; *Calendar of the Laing Charters*, ed J Anderson (Edinburgh, 1899), no 1098.
19   *RSS*, vi, no 2344.
20   *RMS*, iv, no 2499; KBR, 121.
21   *KBR*, 82.
22   *KBR*, 82, 106, 117, 78, 125; MS Burgh Court Books (1.6.3), 4 May 1590; (1.6.4), 10 October 1597; for example.
23   MS Burgh Court Books (1.6.3), May 1595; (1.6.4), 31 May 1596 and 16 May 1597.
24   Irvine, *Kirkcaldy Old Parish Church*, 2, 4, 6.
25   *KBR*, 11, 99, 107.
26   *KBR*, 71, 73, 117–18.
27   W Stevenson, *The Presbyterie Booke of Kirkcaldie* (Kirkcaldy, 1990), 95–6.

area 5 49

Oswald's Wynd / Townsend Place / Coal Wynd / High Street / Port Brae **figure 15**

description

This, one of the smallest of the six arbitrary areas, is bounded by Oswald's Wynd to the south, High Street and Port Brae to the east, Coal Wynd to the north and Townsend Place to the west. Hill Place sub-divides this area into two smaller units.

The area to the west of Hill Place is largely open ground, comprising two car parks, to the north and south respectively, and some large private gardens associated with residential housing fronting onto Townsend Place. The car park at the north end is temporary.

Hill Place itself is unsurfaced, wide at the south end, and narrowing considerably towards the northern end. The properties that front onto the High Street continue up to Hill Place, making them perhaps the best preserved burgage plots in the medieval core of the town, but of uncertain date. The walls at the western end of some of these plots contain the remains of nineteenth-century buildings which once fronted onto Hill Place, and they are depicted on both the maps of Moore (1809) and Wood (1824) **figure 19**.

The rise in ground level from the High Street frontage to the rear of these plots is approximately 10 m; it contains at least two visible terraces, cut into the slope.

A new road scheme has altered the appearance of the north end of this area over recent years. Dunnikier Road has been extended southwards to join with Port Brae, cutting across Coal Wynd, and the junction with the High Street widened. Two car parks have since been constructed, one on either side of the new road. As a result, the High Street frontage in this area has disappeared and, with it, Coldwell Wynd and Stewart's Lane.

The north-west corner of this area, along the Coal Wynd frontage, has also seen some new housing development in recent years.

historical background

Oswald's Wynd, the southern limit to this area, was once called Dishington's Wynd. Sometime after 1820 it was renamed Oswald's Wynd after Sir John Oswald. He had built a town house here, Old Dunnikier House, in the late seventeenth century, in order to meet the residential qualification for members of the town council, residents of Pathhead being debarred from such honour in Kirkcaldy **figure 16**.

---

previous archaeological work

To date, there has been no archaeological work carried out in this area.

chance finds

High Street NT 2791 9101–2832 9177 **G**
Stone coffins, human remains, sculptured arms and inscriptions were discovered in different places by workmen digging foundations in the nineteenth century. They furnish grounds for supposing that a religious house must at one time have stood on the west side of the High Street. *NSA*, ix, 748.

bore-hole surveys

Oswald's Wynd / Hill Place **C**
In advance of car parking in 1980, between 0.30 and 0.80 m of 'fill' was recorded.

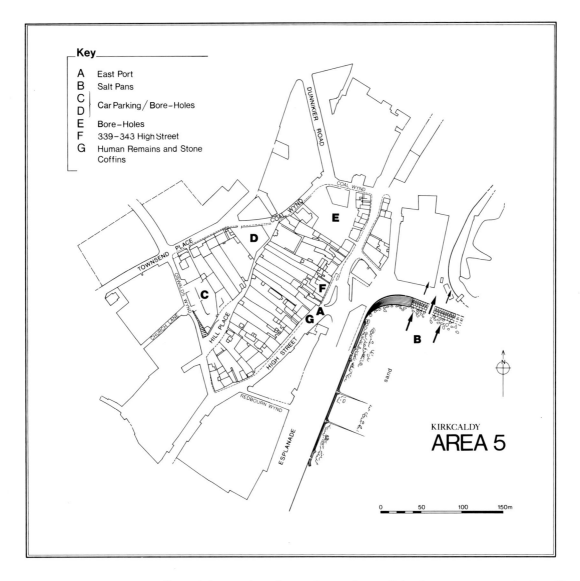

Key

A East Port
B Salt Pans
C
D ⎫ Car Parking / Bore-Holes
E Bore-Holes
F 339–343 High Street
G Human Remains and Stone
   Coffins

KIRKCALDY
AREA 5

0   50   100   150m

figure 15

Area 5

history

Beyond the wynd, to the north, stood one of the three town ports, the East Port **A**. Precisely where this port stood is not known, but it can safely be assumed to have been in the area now called Port Brae.

Ports, or gates, usually simple wooden barresses, were common features in medieval burghs. Their primary function was to monitor access to the burgh. In particular they controlled entrance to the burgh market, the use of which demanded the payment of a toll, or tax, at the port or at the tolbooth (*see* p 30), and excluded potential carriers of plague during outbreaks of the 'pestilence' or 'pest'. In 1585, during a plague scare, it was

archaeology

Coal Wynd / Hill Place **D**
'Fills' ranging from 0.35 m to 1.70 m. were recorded, including ash, rubble and some organic matter, during a bore-hole survey in 1993–4, in advance of the building of a car park.

Port Brae / High Street, 1982 **E**
A bore-hole survey was carried out on the line of a new road joining the High Street at Port Brae with Dunnikier Road. Up to 2.40 m of 'fill' was recorded, comprising rubble, sand, ash, gravel and clay.

future development

No specific development has been proposed for this area in the finalised Local Plan, but land has been reserved in the long term for car parking facilities at Hill Place.

figure 16

Old Dunnikier House

*Kirkcaldy Museum
and Art Gallery*

decided that, apart from parishioners who were permitted to enter the burgh at the Kirk Wynd Port, all strangers were to be denied access by the West Port and were to approach the town by the East Port for scrutiny.[1] Ports were usually set in walls surrounding the town, but most Scottish burghs, Kirkcaldy included, did not have stone encircling walls, relying for a measure of security on small, probably wooden, fences at the end of burgage plots. In all probability, although to date there is no evidence, a simple dyke passed from the shore to the East Port, and from there to the rear of the burgage plots to the west of High Street. There is no evidence, archaeological or documentary, of ditching, as is found in some burghs.

Beyond the port there are several listed buildings. The most significant is 339–343 High Street (*see* p 61).[2] Its importance is based not merely on its architectural merit and interest, and on the archaeological features contained within the structure, but also on what its site tells of Kirkcaldy. Clearly by the late sixteenth century, when this house was built, the burgh had expanded beyond the traditional confines of the town ports. The attraction of the harbour area and its associated facilities as a residential area for both merchants and wealthy mariners at this time is confirmed by the sixteenth- and

history   seventeenth-century owners of this property. The burgage plots in this area of the town

archaeology   archaeological porential **figure 18**

Without any previous work as a guide, the archaeological potential for this area is difficult to gauge accurately. As with Areas 3 and 4, it would seem likely that the narrow strip along the western frontage of the High Street offers the most potential, and this is perhaps confirmed by the survival of the sixteenth-century dwelling house at 339–343 High Street **F** (*see* p 63).

A full study of the nature of cellarage on the High Street was beyond the scope of this survey, but approximately half is thought to be cellared.

Visual examination, together with a cartographic study, indicates that the area between the High Street and Hill Place has so far escaped even nineteenth-century development and therefore offers potential for the survival of archaeological deposits. On the ground, at least, the burgage plots here are the best preserved in the burgh. The question is whether these plots originally extended as far west as they do now, making them easily

52

tend to be broader than within the central core, and this, too, would attract prestigious building. Burgage plots in this area may be viewed clearly on nineteenth-century paintings and photographs, and are still largely traceable on the ground today.

The lie of the land at Port Brae (*see* p 7) inevitably forced the thoroughfare to curve down towards the sea. In conseqence, there was little space for building on the sea side of Port Brae. Indeed, at this point the thoroughfare became only 11 ft 9 ins (3.5 m) wide.[3] Kirkcaldy records refer to a haven, as well as a harbour (*see* pp 53–6). The stretch of water off-shore at this point may well be the haven, near to and closely associated with the harbour (*see* p 55), as records in 1601 suggest that the 'old haven' lay a little south of the harbour **figure 7**.[4]

On the shore nearby were Kirkcaldy's salt-pans **B**. By the early 1570s there were twenty-eight, owned by seven different owners. These formed a vital part of the town's economy for centuries, but their site is now lost below modern harbour works (*see* p 15).

Coal Wynd, which terminates this block, is one of several small wynds giving access to the harbour. This particular wynd is so called as it was used to transport coal from the Lina Pit.

notes

history

1   *KBR*, 11, 99, 107.
2   Comprehensive details of this house and the current restoration work by Scottish Historic Buildings Trust are contained in R Scrimgeour, 'Nos 339–343 High Street, Kirkcaldy: Record and Analysis for the Scottish Historic Buildings Trust' (Kirkcaldy, 1993).
3   Richard Moore, 'Plan of the Royal Burgh of Kirkcaldy' (Abbotshall, 1809).
4   MS Burgh Court Book (1.6.5), 26 April 1601.

archaeology

the longest on the west side of the High Street. If not, they must represent a later development of the medieval burgh.

The bore-hole surveys have not been undertaken in that part of in that part of the area with perhaps the most archaeological potential. Where carried out, they encountered mostly rubble, where nineteenth-century buildings had been demolished to make way for road widening and car parks. However, the organic material recorded in the bore-holes at **B** is interesting. Whether this represents medieval deposits is uncertain but is perhaps unlikely, given its location some distance from the High Street frontage.

A study of the topography, or physical setting, of the burgh for this survey (*see* pp 5–8) has suggested that the westward development of the medieval burgh was constricted by the slope that rises westwards from the High Street—a rise of up to 10 m in places over a distance of less than 150 m. Therefore, it would seem that the medieval settlement in this part of the town (*see also* Areas 3 and 5) originally comprised a narrow strip along the west side of the High Street **figure 3**.

Monitoring of development here may offer the opportunity to answer a range of archaeological questions, not only about the nature of the structures on the frontage but also about the chronology of the development of this part of the burgh. More specifically, the nature of usage of the backlands, and their contrast with those on the seaward side of the High Street, needs to be assessed. The nature of the property boundaries at the end of the rigs that marked the western limit of the burgh also needs to be assessed. Finally, the nature and date of the burgage plots, possibly the largest in the burgh and part of a later development, extending westwards from the High Street frontage, need to be established.

The discovery of the sculptured arms and inscriptions with the stone coffins and human remains implies that these are probably relatively late in date. However, without an accurate location or description of the finds, little more can be said concerning the possible existence of a religious house on the west side of the High Street.

area 6   53

harbour/High Street/Sailors' Walk/Dunnikier Road/St Mary's Road **figure 17**

description

This area lies outwith the core of the medieval burgh of Kirkcaldy, and mostly within the neighbouring burgh of Pathhead. Therefore fieldwork, in terms of identifying archaeological potential, was limited to the area around the harbour, and Sailors' Walk in particular. The historical evidence, however, covers a slightly wider area, taking in some of the surviving buildings in Pathhead.

The High Street continues northwards from Port Brae, past the harbour to the east and onwards up the hill, along The Path, towards Pathhead.

The section of the High Street opposite the main dock of the harbour is also known as 'Sailors' Walk'; it contains a fine seventeenth-century dwelling house, 443–447 High Street **E** (*see* pp 61–2), and other eighteenth-century buildings. Three narrow vennels— Coal Wynd, Malcolm's Wynd and Fish Wynd—run westwards from the High Street. Waste ground lies behind much of this frontage.

historical background

Although technically outwith the medieval bounds of Kirkcaldy burgh, this area is highly significant historically, and possibly archaeologically. It has been mooted that first settlement in Kirkcaldy was at and around the mouth of the East Burn (*see* p 12).

This area also embraces one of the significant assets of Kirkcaldy from medieval times: its harbour **figure 7**. How early Kirkcaldy had a harbour is not known, but there was one in existence by 1451 when it is referred to in a charter between the abbot of Dunfermline and the burgesses of Kirkcaldy.[1] Whether this early harbour was at the mouth of the East Burn, the site of the later harbour works, is unclear. It would seem very probable, however, as even though there was a facility for beaching boats on the sands to the south of East Burn, a trading settlement such as Kirkcaldy, exporting and importing from the Low Countries, England and the Baltic (*see* pp 13,15), would have needed the greater protection of a sheltered inlet to moor boats and to land goods. The mouth of the East Burn would have been a natural place to commence primitive harbour works. By 1536 it was sufficiently functional for Kirkcaldy harbour to be the departure point for James V's visit to France.[2]

previous archaeological work

Priory Park NT *2837 9235* **C**
A cist burial was discovered during the digging of foundation trenches for a housing development. The cist comprised four side slabs, with a covering lid displaced by the on-site machinery. The foot stone appeared to have been dressed. The inhumation, aligned east to west with the head to the west, was laid on a bed of small, rounded pebbles **figure 4**. There was no evidence of any grave goods, but fragments of calcined animal bone were found in the chest area. Examination of the skeleton revealed the burial to be of a young female, aged between 25 and 30, with some bones showing signs of repetitive strain injuries. *DES* (1992), 30.

St Mary's Well, Pathhead NT *2840 9229* **D**
Supposed site of a well, though no trace of any structure survives today.

chance finds

No chance finds have been reported for this area.

54

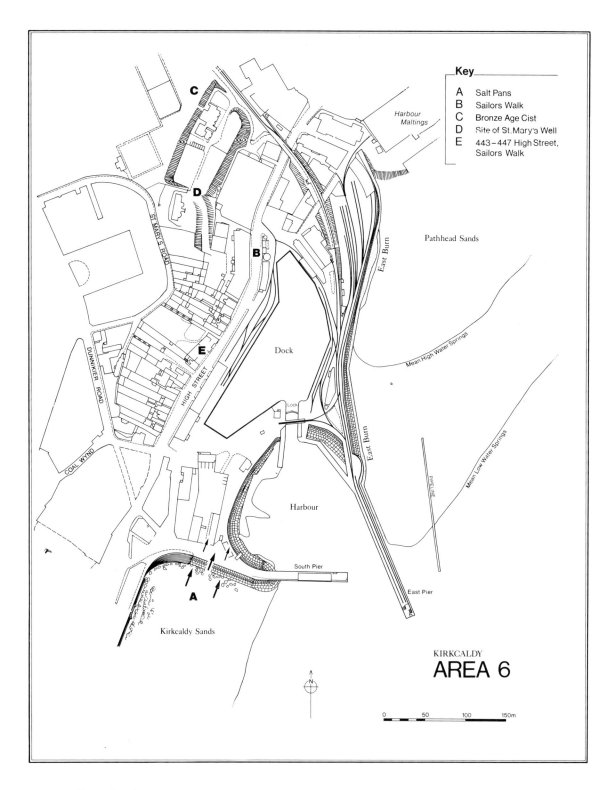

figure 17

Area 6

The burgh records highlight the attention the townspeople gave to the maintenance and upgrading of the harbour, which had been reported in 1544 as having a pier, a very good landing with boats at 'full see' and a good road within half a mile of the shore.[3] By 1567, four harbour masters were employed. Apart from overseeing the fabric of the harbour, they levied fines on those who threw their ballast into the harbour, and charged strangers who overwintered: 10s for a ship and 5s for a boat.[4]

The last decade of the sixteenth century was a time of constant consultation concerning the building work at the harbour. In 1589 'the haill commountie' met in the kirk to lay down a scheme for building a totally new pier and harbour at the Monkcraig.[5] This was to be a costly venture, so alternative possibilities, such as merely repairing the pier and harbour, were discussed over a number of years. It was ultimately decided that the existing pier and harbour works were to be extended and partially replaced, by the addition of a pier and harbour at the Monkcraig.[6] To this end, six oak trees were to be set into the Monkcraig for mooring ships, an option first mooted in 1592.[7] Funding for this project was to be assisted by the raising of taxes on certain commodities, permission for which was given by the Convention of Royal Burghs in 1592 and again in 1596.[8] This was renewed for a further seven years in 1599.[9] By 1600 the work on the new pier was sufficiently well advanced for a decision to be made that the old pier should be dismantled and the wood put to use elsewhere at the expense of the townspeople.[10] Such expensive, radical upgrading and extension work is testament to the importance of the town's harbour and the value of its coal and salt exports (*see* pp 13,15).

This concern to maintain the harbour and its associated haven and pier continued throughout the seventeenth century. By 1663 several breaches had appeared in the new harbour works, requiring repair work.[11] To assist in maintenance, it was decided in 1675 to call for financial assistance from neighbouring burghs, presumably because they, too, benefited from an efficiently functioning harbour at Kirkcaldy.[12] By 1676 extension work was such that the harbour works could specifically be called two harbours, the 'old' and the 'new', as it was laid down that there was to be no tipping of ballast between the old and new harbours.[13] The pier was also 'perfyted' in 1679.[14]

history

archaeology

future development

No specific development has been proposed for this area in the finalised Local Plan, but the area around the harbour is viewed as presenting a long-term opportunity for redevelopment.

archaeological potential **figure 18**

Only a small portion within this area has been studied in any detail, so comments on the archaeological potential have been limited to the High Street/Sailors' Walk area.

A cartographic study of the area, from Coal Wynd northwards to the East Burn, indicates that, as with Area 5, the burgage plots here are, on the whole, larger than elsewhere in the town. This implies that this area may have been a later suburb.

The lack of any previous work in this area, together with the absence of chance finds and engineers' bore-holes, makes accurate assessment of its potential difficult. However, the preservation of the seventeenth- and eighteenth-century frontage along this section of the High Street suggests that this area, and the area immediately behind the frontage, do have some archaeological potential.

Monitoring of development here may offer the opportunity to answer a range of archaeological questions, not only about the nature of the structures on the frontage but also about the chronology of the development of this part of the burgh. Its position, outside the East Port, suggests that this area, although it contains some of the earliest surviving standing buildings in the town, was a later suburb, which developed as a result of the success of the harbour in the sixteenth and seventeenth centuries.

Much of the eighteenth century was spent fighting storm damage and failing trade figures (*see* pp 17–18). Considerable destruction resulted from a violent storm in 1717, but not until 1752 was a decision made to build a west pier. The purpose of this was not only to protect the harbour which, it was said, filled with sand and flotsam during storms, but also to protect the salt-pans to the south of the harbour.[15] Four years later, an addition of between thirty and forty feet (9 to 12 m) was made to the west pier.[16] Kirkcaldy was not, however, to see a true regeneration in the growth of its harbour until towards the turn of the century, with shipbuilding and manufacturing boosting its economy (*see* pp 18–19). By 1797, the deepening of a new basin was authorised,[17] and the nineteenth century was to bring extensive improvements to the harbour basin, works and docks. The connection of the railway to the harbour in 1849 further ensured that Kirkcaldy could benefit from its site as an east coast port with internal and overseas contacts.

To the south of the harbour, on the shore, were sited Kirkcaldy's salt-pans **A**, **figure 19**). By the early 1570s there were twenty-eight, owned by seven different owners, including the family of Weymss of Bogie. These formed a vital part of the town's economy for centuries, but their site is now lost below modern harbour works (*see* p 15).

Leading from the harbour area were several wynds, which served to transport goods to and from the harbour. Most have now disappeared with redevelopment. Coal Wynd and Fish Wynd are two remnants (*see* pp 71, 72). Beside the harbour stood associated buildings, three of which remain standing. Particularly to be noted are Harbour House, the old nineteenth-century customs house, and nearby 443–447 High Street, Sailors' Walk **B** (*see* pp 61–2).

The road from the harbour was little more than a muddy track until well into the nineteenth century. It led north, along the Path, to the East Bridge and East Mill, past Hutchison's House and Dunnikier House (*see* p 71), to Pathhead, a burgh with close associations, but independent of Kirkcaldy until 1876 (*see* p 19). Ravenscraig Castle, on the coast north of Kirkcaldy harbour, outwith the medieval burgh and with closer links with nearby Dysart, had, however, an impact on Kirkcaldy and its burgesses, and, indeed, the entire locality. The castle was at times the temporary residence of kings, and perhaps the first castle in Scotland to have been built for firearm defence (*see* pp 64–5).[18]

history

archaeology

The exact position of the original harbour may perhaps never be confirmed, since the extension of the current harbour in the nineteenth century has no doubt removed most, perhaps all, traces of earlier structures, and timber wharves in particular. Although boats could easily have been simply dragged up on the sands, the area around the East Burn must be a candidate for the site of the earliest harbour (*see* p 12).

Finally, the discovery of the Bronze Age cist burial within this block is a clear indicator of the potential for prehistoric archaeological remains on the west side of the High Street, and a testament to the attractiveness of the area in prehistory.

1   *Dunf Reg*, no 432.
2   Lockhart, *Kirkcaldy Burgh and
     Harbour, 1.*
3   *Hamilton Papers*, ii, 714.
4   Lockhart, *Kirkcaldy Burgh and
     Harbour*, 2.
5   MS Burgh Court Book (1.6.2), 13
     October 1589.
6   MS Burgh Court Books (1.6.3) 15
     May 1592; (1.6.4), 31 May 1596,
     11 October 1596, 11 April 1597,
     16 May 1597; (1.6.5), 9 October
     1598, 15 January 1599.
7   MS Burgh Court Book (1.6.3), 15
     May 1592.
8   *RCRB*, i, 389, 489.
9   *RCRB*, ii, 55.
10 MS Burgh Court Book (1.6.5), 12
     January 1601.

11 *KBR*, 178.
12 *KBR*, 206.
13 *KBR*, 206.
14 *KBR*, 208.
15 Lockhart, *Kirkcaldy Burgh and
     Harbour, passim.*
16 *Ibid.*
17 *Ibid.*
18 G Stell, 'Late medieval defences in
     Scotland', in D H Caldwell (ed),
     *Scottish Weapons and Fortifications,
     1100–1800* (Edinburgh, 1981),
     29; W D Simpson, *Ravenscraig
     Castle* (Aberdeen University
     Studies, no 115), *passim*; W D
     Simpson, *Ravenscraig Castle*
     (Transactions of the Glasgow
     Archaeological Society), new ser,
     viii, pt 4, 46–55.

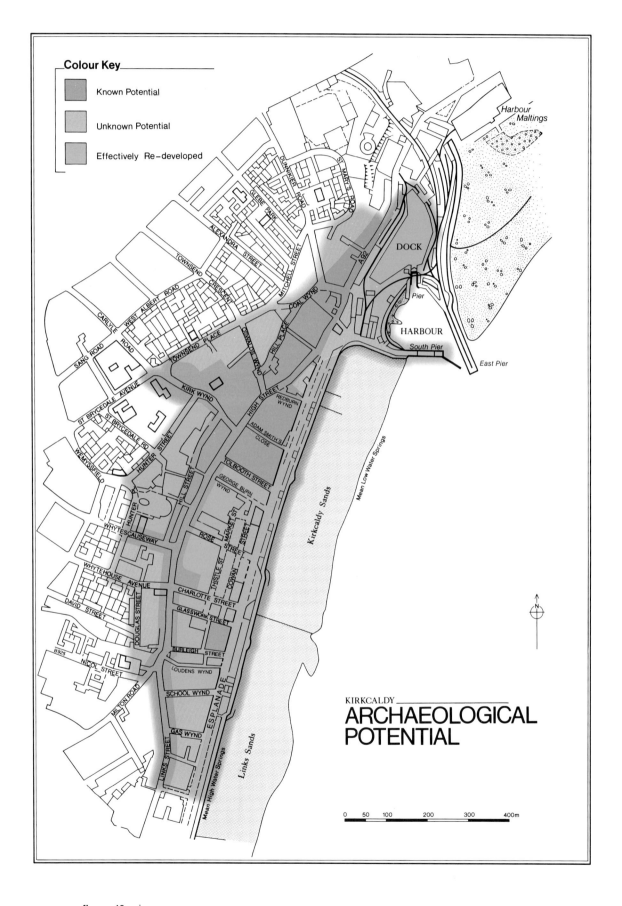

58

Colour Key

Known Potential

Unknown Potential

Effectively Re-developed

KIRKCALDY
ARCHAEOLOGICAL POTENTIAL

figure 18

archaeological

potential

the archaeological potential of Kirkcaldy a summary **figure 18**   59

an overview

On present evidence, it must be admitted that the overall potential for the survival of
archaeological deposits within the medieval core of Kirkcaldy is perhaps limited.
Nevertheless, routine monitoring and excavations in many other Scottish towns, especially
Perth and Aberdeen but also in some smaller towns, have demonstrated that medieval and
later archaeological remains do often survive beneath a modern street frontage.
Therefore, the site of any proposed ground disturbance or development along the main
street frontages in Kirkcaldy, and High Street and Kirk Wynd in particular, must be
accorded a high archaeological priority, and arrangements made for the site to be
assessed, monitored and, if necessary, excavated in advance of the development scheme.
Similarly, any proposed ground disturbance of the streets and wynds themselves (for
instance, for essential repairs, access to services, or environmental improvements) should
also be monitored routinely, because the remains of some of the most important features
of the medieval townscape may be sealed beneath them—the ports, tolbooth and market
cross—of which no archaeological evidence at all has yet been found.

To date, there have been remarkably few opportunities for archaeological investigation
in Kirkcaldy. Of necessity therefore, this assessment of the archaeological potential has
been made in the almost complete absence of evidence from previous archaeological work
in the town. Engineers' bore holes have provided some additional information but have
proved to be of limited value overall. Thus, the conclusions and recommendations
expressed here should be regarded as provisional; this survey will require periodic review
in the light of results from any future campaigns of archaeological fieldwork (assessment,
monitoring and excavation), and from other types of sub-surface investigations.

It is important to stress here that the survey area was limited to the core of historic
(medieval) Kirkcaldy. There is a recognised, though unquantifiable, potential for the
discovery of prehistoric and Roman archaeological remains, both within and outwith the
confines of the historic burgh. This potential is *not* considered or shown on **figure 18**.

Finally, the potential for archaeological features and deposits to be preserved both
beneath the floors and within the structures of historic standing buildings in Kirkcaldy (pp
61–5) must not be forgotten. That such a potential exists was most recently demonstrated
in the restoration work on the sixteenth-century house at 339–343 High Street. The
archaeological potential of Kirkcaldy's standing buildings is also *not* shown on **figure 18**,
but the potential of individual historic buildings is considered in the next section.

Turning to the specific areas of Kirkcaldy (as identified in this survey), most of Areas 1,
4 and 5, and part of Area 6, appear to offer archaeological potential, with Areas 1 and 5
clearly promising the best preserved backlands. Areas 2 and 3 on the other hand appear
overall to offer low archaeological potential, with large parts of them effectively
redeveloped. However, it must be expected that pockets of archaeological deposits, some
perhaps sizeable, could be preserved even within areas identified generally as having low
(or unknown) potential. **figure 18** distinguishes between areas of known potential (shaded
green) and unknown potential (shaded lighter green). **All green areas should be treated as
potentially archaeologically sensitive**. Effectively redeveloped areas (shaded blue) are
probably archaeologically sterile.

area 1

Area 1, together with Area 5, perhaps best reflects the medieval character of the town.
There is little doubt, despite the limited opportunities so far presented for archaeological
investigation, that Area 1 offers archaeological potential. Of particular importance are the
High Street frontage and the backlands to the south of Redburn Wynd. Tolbooth Street,
although itself an eighteenth-century insertion, may also seal earlier, possibly medieval,
burgage plots.

area 2

In view of the scale of development in recent years in this area and the disappearance of identifiable properties extending from the High Street eastwards, it would seem unlikely that archaeological deposits survive to any great extent within Area 2, except possibly on the High Street frontage itself. Therefore, the potential here is seen as generally low.

area 3

A study of the physical setting of the burgh for this survey (*see* pp 5–8) has suggested that the westward development of the medieval burgh was constricted by the slope that rises westwards from the High Street. It would seem then that medieval settlement in this part of the town was most probably located in a narrow strip along the west of the High Street. The archaeological potential of Area 3 is therefore centred on the narrow strip along the western frontage of the High Street.

area 4

The northern section of this area contains a high proportion of open ground and has escaped much of the more recent redevelopment of the town. At first sight therefore, this area seems to offer good archaeological potential. However, this observation must be balanced against the disappointing results of recent archaeological work at Seaview House, which suggested that this westernmost part of the town may have been largely open ground throughout its history, including in the medieval period. If this is indeed the case, few features of significance may ever have existed here.

The archaeological potential of Area 4 is therefore thought to be centred on the narrow strip along the western frontage of the High Street, along both frontages of Kirk Wynd and in the area around the parish church.

area 5

Without any previous work as a guide, it is very difficult to guage the archaeological potential of this area accurately. As with Areas 3 and 4, it would seem likely that the narrow strip along the western frontage of the High Street offers the most potential, an hypothesis which is supported by the survival of the sixteenth-century dwelling house at 339–343 High Street. Visual examination, together with a cartographic study, indicate that the area between the High Street and Hill Place has so far escaped even nineteenth-century development and, therefore, may also offer high potential for the survival of archaeological deposits. On the ground, at least, the burgage plots here are the best preserved in the burgh. However, they may represent a later development of the medieval burgh.

area 6

Only a small part of this area has been studied in any detail. Comments on the archaeological potential have been limited to the High Street/Sailors' Walk area.

The lack of any previous archaeological work in Area 6, together with the absence of any chance finds or engineers' bore holes, make an accurate assessment difficult. However, the preservation of the seventeenth- and eighteenth-century frontage along this section of the High Street suggests that this area at least, and the area immediately behind the frontage, has some archaeological potential.

Several historic standing buildings survive, in part or in whole, and, although only one is identifiably medieval, these do provide some physical clues to Kirkcaldy's history. Archaeological material is likely to be preserved both beneath and within these standing buildings and may survive either as a sequence of floor levels or as deposits which predate the construction of the buildings themselves, or concealed within the upstanding structure.

The *tower of St Bryce Church* is probably the sole pre-Reformation remnant in the town, the oldest section of the western tower being probably of mid fifteenth-century origin (*see* **figure 14**). A church has stood on this site since at least 1244; the first known here had a David de Bernham dedication. At the head of Kirk Wynd, on a hill overlooking the High Street, its commanding position still reflects its role in the community—a focal point for the spiritual well-being of the town, near, but outwith, the centre of settlement (*see* pp 15–16). Although major development here is unlikely, alterations within the standing building or in the grounds of the church, for example the insertion of new services, may reveal the remains of earlier structures and possibly traces of the thirteenth-century church.

To the east of the town are two important buildings (*see* p 45).

339–343 High Street is a sixteenth-century dwelling of significance, currently undergoing restoration by the Scottish Historic Buildings Trust. A three-storeyed building with a floored roof-space, its front exterior has undergone little change, other than new windows and doors being inserted and older ones blocked up, although the shops on the frontage are a major disruption. Originally, an internal stone spiral staircase was sited at the front of the house; the ground floor probably contained a kitchen at the east end; the first storey housed a large central hall with a massive fireplace and a chamber at each end; the second floor was probably of similar design. The original decorations also indicate that this was a dwelling of substance. The soffits of the second floor joists and boards were adorned with tempera painted designs, and there were pictorial decorations on the plastered walls, two of which at least survive—a lion, and a ship in full sail. In keeping with its continuing importance, the interior was modernised, possibly in the 1670s, with the addition of wooden panelling on internal partitions, and lath-and-plaster ceilings and cornices, the first floor ceilings being embellished with deep covings and decorative bands, roses and putti. Later internal changes altered its character: the front stair was taken down and a rear external staircase substituted; a pend was inserted right through the building; and there was a realignment of some rooms. External alterations created a west wing to the rear and added various outbuildings. This restoration project is a good example of the archaeological potential of historic standing buildings.

443–447 High Street (Sailors' Walk) may have originated as two dwellings. A characteristic seventeenth-century block, it probably incorporated an earlier building. Gables project to front and rear, the western gable being crow-stepped and corbelled out over the ground floor, while the roofs are pantiled, perhaps reflecting trading contacts with the Low Countries. In due course the building came to be divided into four dwellings. One of these, the East House, is approached by a turnpike staircase, and incorporates two interesting apartments. A rear room is finely panelled; another has a painted wooden ceiling, probably of early seventeenth-century origin, with arabesques and birds' and animals' heads on the boards, and biblical texts on the beams. An inscribed lintel over a fireplace bears the date 1676. A repositioned stone tablet bears the arms of Charles II. This was originally located on the east elevation.

Both of these buildings throw light on Kirkcaldy's past. Their position outside the East Port and near the harbour suggests that, as has been proved for 339–343 High Street, both dwellings were the homes of wealthy merchants or shipowners. Their sites offered ready access to the port and perhaps an oversight of the owners' ships. (Could it be that the ship painting in 339–343 High Street was an illustration of the owner's own ship?) It is unlikely that these were the only prestigious dwellings in this area of the town. Development outwith the town port suggests that this suburb was becoming desirable in the sixteenth and seventeenth centuries because of the increasing economic importance of Kirkcaldy's harbour, in spite of the hubbub and dirt associated with a port. Cartographic evidence, moreover, indicates that burgage plots were wider here than in the central core

62

figure 19

Plan of the town of
Kirkcaldy by John
Wood, 1824

*National Library of
Scotland map room*

of the town, which would also have attracted, and might indicate, prestigious building. The later subdivision of both houses, certainly by the early nineteenth century, into a number of tenements is partly a reflection of the area becoming socially less desirable. Manufacturing premises moved in towards the harbour region, and the wealthier elements of society opted to move to quieter suburbs, further removed from the industrial core of Kirkcaldy.

Any refurbishment to these two standing buildings, the ground to the rear of the properties and the pend at *339–343 High Street*, such as the insertion of new services, new floors or re-surfacing, would have archaeological implications. This might reveal, for example, successive floor levels associated with early phases of the buildings, or secondary structures attached to the rear of the properties. As both these buildings are situated outside the northern limit of the medieval burgh, any archaeological deposits that can be demonstrated to predate the construction of the standing building would also provide a date for the establishment of what may be a later suburb.

Four buildings in the heart of the burgh give an insight into central Kirkcaldy in the seventeenth and eighteenth centuries.

34–36 Kirk Wynd (Andersoune's House) is a somewhat altered, probably partly early eighteenth-century dwelling house, although the date 1637 on the door lintel would suggest that sections of the house, at least, are earlier (*see* **figure 14**). Named after Matthew Anderson, a local meal dealer and maltster as well as a ruling elder in the parish church, the house is crow-stepped with a lean-to wing projecting onto the street.

17 Tolbooth Street is a pantiled, eighteenth-century dwelling comprising two storeys and an attic.

23/25 Tolbooth Street, its near neighbour, is a three-storeyed, rubble-built dwelling with moulded door frames bearing the date 1785.

219 High Street to 3/7 Kirk Wynd standing on the corner of High Street and Kirk Wynd is a derelict building with crow-stepped gables, the only surviving such dwelling on the High Street. It still reveals eighteenth-century features, in spite of its poor state (*see* **figure 14**).

All of these dwellings were in the traditional prime site of the medieval burgh: near the market centre and the market cross in the High Street. They are fair reflections of quality housing for important burgesses in the heart of the town in the seventeenth and eighteenth centuries. Many of the buildings lining the High Street display a distinguished architectural character that developed in the commercial and banking centre in the late eighteenth and early nineteenth century, when Kirkcaldy was a prosperous manufacturing town.

Street frontages have, in the light of recent excavations, been the most rewarding in terms of the preservation of archaeological deposits, despite the problem of cellarage. Although there has been no opportunity to examine the High Street frontage or any of the other main street frontages in Kirkcaldy, evidence of medieval structures in the form of post-holes and floor surfaces may be expected, sealed beneath the nineteenth-century standing buildings. Recent excavations in Perth, Dunfermline and Arbroath have also shown that the width and alignment of the main streets in the burgh have changed over the centuries. Earlier cobbled street surfaces and contemporary buildings have been preserved up to three or four metres behind the modern street frontage. This may be the case in Kirkcaldy.

193–199 High Street, 191 High Street and *148–156 High Street*, for example, are all early nineteenth-century in origin. They have interesting columned and pillared doorways, that at 148–156 being most impressive, with classic Doric column doorpieces with thistles carved into the pediments. Between the doorways of 148–156 High Street is a pend leading to a courtyard and an 1830 building with an ornate pediment over the door and two Doric columns on either side of the doorway. This was built to house a bank, as were 148–156 High Street and 191 High Street. *224–226 High Street* was also built as a bank in 1833 by William Burn, and has impressive first-floor windows and a balustraded cornice with gargoyle heads. *133–135 High Street* was similarly built as the Glasgow Bank, in *c* 1835. This building also displays a balustraded cornice.

Evidence of other early nineteenth-century buildings can still be seen, such as in the block of property at *51–59 High Street*, although it reveals less ornamentation than the impressive banking structures. *263–265 High Street* is a four-storeyed, five-windowed, painted ashlar-fronted building with a deep wood modillioned cornice of *c* 1800. *267–271 High Street* is of similar date, but a plainer version of its neighbour. They all serve to illustrate the standing of the burgh in the early nineteenth century.

At the eastern, harbour end of the town, two standing buildings reflect the tone of the area in the late eighteenth and early nineteenth centuries. At *399 High Street* is one of the oldest licensed premises in Kirkcaldy. Built around 1770, it was once called 'The Focsle', and would be typical of many such public houses that crowded around the port area. Close by the harbour, at *427–431 High Street*, approached by a lane, is the early nineteenth-century Harbour House, the old customs house, a two-storey and basement building with a pedimented wall-head gable.

Although not technically within the old Kirkcaldy burgh, two standing dwellings in Pathhead reflect the quality building that could result from local wealth. *Dunnikier House* or *Path House*, in Nether Street, was built by John Watson in 1692, but was soon sold to the Oswald family who had important connections with Kirkcaldy. An L-plan, three-storeyed, harled building, it has a number of interesting architectural features including scrolled skewputs at the base of the gables and a double wall sundial. The circular tower in the re-entrant angle was inserted in the late nineteenth century.

Hutchison's House stands nearby on the Path. Erected in 1793 by one Spiers who owned a distillery at the nearby East Bridge, it is an impressive building, displaying the wealth of the owner, with a pedimented façade and elliptical fanlight. To the south of the dwelling is a round gin house, originally used for horses to work a threshing mill.

A further building which reflects the prestige of certain Kirkcaldy residents is at Hunter Hospital in Hunter Street. The central portion is *St Brycedale House*, a smart residence built for George Heggie in 1786. It is harled with ashlar belt courses, with centre bows at front and back, the front one being carried on a Roman doric portico.

Also technically outwith Kirkcaldy burgh, but with strong ties to their northerly neighbour, are three buildings in Linktown.

Bethelfield Church, Nicol Street, built in 1830–1 and opened in 1831, is a rectangular classic Secession church. Nearby, a dwelling house at *44 Nicol Street*, once called Abbotshall House, was built about 1800. It later functioned as the office for Halley's dyeworks, which occupied many of the buildings of the first steam-powered mill in Kirkcaldy, the Abbotshall linen works. Although restored, the façade and the pillared entrance still reveal a substantial dwelling house, typical of the early nineteenth century. Next door, *46 Nicol Street*, built in 1820, was once the home of John Methven, the Links Pottery owner. Nicol Street was originally known as Newton, and was built up from around 1790 on feus granted by the Fergusons of Raith. Although housing textile mills, it was still, in the nineteenth century, considered a sufficiently commodious area for the dwellings of wealthy factory owners, as indicated by these properties.

Dominating the northern reaches of the town is *Ravenscraig Castle*. Outwith the boundaries of medieval Kirkcaldy, and with stronger links with Dysart, the castle still had a significant impact on Kirkcaldy. Built on a promontory, jutting eighty feet high above Kirkcaldy Bay, with a sheer face to the west and a more irregular shelving to the east, the castle stands in a seemingly impregnable position from the sea. During the fifteenth century the crown was showing increasing concern for littoral defence, both against piracy and English aggression. In 1460, therefore, James II commenced the building of the castle, in such a situation that it could command the upper reaches of the Forth and protect the important port of Dysart, and also, in the event, the small harbour of Kirkcaldy. Work continued after the death of the king that year, with the intention that the castle should be completed as a dower house for his widow, Mary of Gueldres. Whether this was achieved is doubtful, much further work being done for the Sinclair family in the sixteenth century. The main accommodation was provided in two towers flanking the base of the triangular promontory, supported by ancillary buildings, with a third tower at the end of the promontory.

The architecture of the standing remains of the castle reveals the response to the threat of bombardment from the sea: the walls of the towers are between 3.3 and 4.4 m in thickness. Gun loops and a gun platform, protected by a curtain wall between the two towers, are an engineering reaction to the threat posed by the new artillery. Ravenscraig Castle may be the first castle in Scotland specifically designed for firearm defence.

Not only did Kirkcaldy benefit from a measure of protection and coastal defence afforded by the nearby castle, but as late medieval castles also served administrative and political purposes, Kirkcaldy was drawn into national events merely by being in the castle's locality. Ravenscraig Castle was the home of Mary of Gueldres until her death in 1463, and although it passed out of royal hands to the Sinclairs in 1470, several royal visitors passed through Kirkcaldy. James V, for example, sailed from Kirkcaldy in 1536 to bring his French wife back to Scotland; a royal charter was issued from Ravenscraig in April 1540; and James VI lodged at the castle in 1598. In due course the castle was deserted, but why or when is not clear. The last chapter in its history was an ignominious one; it probably functioned as quarters for troops during the Cromwellian occupation of Fife in 1651.

suggested avenues for further work

pp 67–69

There are certain areas of research which of necessity have not been pursued in this report, but consideration of the following sources might shed more light on historic Kirkcaldy.

For instance, the importance of **Kirkcaldy harbour**—which played a crucial role in the history of the town—is reflected in the primary source material. The attention given to repairing, and even totally re-building harbour works as early as the late sixteenth century, has been noted elsewhere (pp 55–6); further research in the burgh records will undoubtedly throw light on the seventeenth-century upgrading of the harbour works and, together with any archaeological evidence, perhaps clarify the relationship between the 'old' and 'new' harbours.

The **maritime history and archaeology** of Kirkcaldy also deserve investigation. The Firth of Forth is, and perhaps always has been, one of the busiest sea-lanes in Scotland. Consequently, the potential for shipwrecks, and therefore maritime archaeology, is considerable. Any wrecks identified in and around Kirkcaldy harbour may shed light not only on the position of the early harbour but also on the nature and extent of Kirkcaldy's shipping industry. This avenue has been largely ignored and, as there is no national database for Scotland, it was felt to be beyond the scope of this project. Potential sources of information include records of the Scottish Office and Admiralty Court.

The wider context of the historic burgh of Kirkcaldy might also be considered in due course. In particular, the **relationship between the burghs** of Kirkcaldy and Dysart, and the

---

archaeological objectives for the future

Preparation of the Kirkcaldy burgh survey has highlighted a number of directions for future archaeological work. These can be broadly divided into management objectives, priorities for future fieldwork, and other areas which merit further research. Any such list cannot be exhaustive but it should cover the main areas of concern in the foreseeable future.

management objectives

1   Wherever possible, it is important to continue to monitor the impact of any development (in its broadest sense) on the potential archaeological resource (the **green areas** on **figure 18**). This will require the routine provision of site-specific desk-based assessments, through to watching briefs, trial excavations and, where necessary, controlled excavation, post-excavation analysis and publication. Over time, the cumulative results will 'calibrate' this assessment of the archaeological potential of the burgh, providing evidence about the burgh's origins, and its physical, economic and social development through the centuries.

2   Developments should similarly be monitored to shed more light on the prehistory of Kirkcaldy (including its possible use as a late Neolithic/Bronze Age funerary landscape), and on its function in the Roman sphere of influence.

3   The degree and nature of cellarage along the High Street was not systematically examined during preparation of this report. About half the properties are thought to be cellared but more accurate information would be most useful to managers/curators of the archaeological resource in assessing the archaeological potential of the main street frontage in the burgh. Files containing this source material are available through Kirkcaldy District Council, Planning and Building Control Departments.

baronial burghs of Linktown and Pathhead, would reward investigation both archaeologically and historically. An equal-handed comparative approach to these neighbouring coastal burghs might prove more informative than a study which concentrates on the hinterland of Kirkcaldy itself.

There are available a number of further documentary sources which might shed more light on historic Kirkcaldy.

repository: Town House, Kirkcaldy
1.1.18 MSS Kirkcaldy Council Minutes.
1.6.11–18 MSS Burgh Court Books of Kirkcaldy (this source was used extensively, but most emphasis was given to the head courts).
1.9.1–6 MSS Trades Council Books.
MSS Kirk Session Records, 1614–1645; 1690 onwards (uncatalogued).
MS Rothes Cartulary, 1627–1902 (uncatalogued).

repository: Scottish Record Office, Edinburgh
Papers of the Oswald of Dunnikier Estate, NRA 1879 (5 chests).
Papers of the Hutcheson family, NRA 3395.
history   Burgh Register of Sasines; List of Sasines 1539–1607, B41/1/1.

---

archaeology

4   Engineers' bore holes offer a convenient glimpse of the depth and nature of sub-surface deposits, man-made or not, ancient and modern. It would be useful if the results obtained from engineers' bore holes in and around the core of the historic burgh could be gradually collected and collated. In the present survey, it proved difficult to access all bore hole results, especially those in the hands of private contractors, and it might be worth considering mechanisms by which such information could more easily (and preferably routinely) be made available to managers/curators of the archaeological resource.

5   Opportunities should continue to be taken to increase public awareness of the potential archaeological interest of Kirkcaldy, both generally and within and beneath historic standing buildings. This survey represents an important first step in this direction.

6   Periodic review and updating of this survey would be desirable to take account of the results of any future archaeological work, and of the comprehensive collection and collation of other types of sub-surface investigations eg. engineers' bore holes, systematic survey of cellarage on the main street frontages etc. In particular, the colour-coded map **figure 18** could perhaps be revised and re-issued at appropriate intervals.

priorities for future fieldwork

So little archaeological work has so far been undertaken in Kirkcaldy that the priorities for future archaeological fieldwork are fairly rudimentary. However, the following priorities should be borne in mind during preparation of future project designs.

1   Define the limits of the medieval burgh and the character and date of any burgh boundaries; in particular, test the hypothesis of this survey that the steep slope to the west of the High Street was a limiting factor in the westward development of the burgh.

2   Identify any sequence of planning in the layout and expansion of the burgh, and determine any variation in street alignment and width.

Protocol Book of Robert French, 1591, NP1/57.
Inventory of the Charter Kist of the Wemyss of Bogie, RH9/4/2.
Register of Testaments, within Commissariot Record of St Andrews, Kirkcaldy parish,
  CC20/4/ .
Sundry burghal charters.

repository: Forbo Nairn Manufacturers Office, Kirkcaldy
Nairn family papers.

repository: St Andrews University
Minute Book of the Prime Gilt Box Society, 1612–1674 (copy).

repository: National Library of Scotland, Edinburgh
Miscellaneous deeds and papers relating to the family of Wemyss of Bogie, 1549–1763.
Accounts, Receipts and Obligations for Lairds of Bogie, coalmasters and saltmasters,
  1660–1718.
Deeds to Sir James Wemyss of Bogie, 1608 and 1616.
Deed relating to Salt-pans, 1647.

history   *Repository: Glenrothes Development Corporation*
Rothes MSS, including 'Questions and answers *re* Lord St Clair's coal, 1730'.

archaeology   3   Assess whether burgage plots to the west of the High Street, at Port Brae, are a later
  development of the medieval burgh, as has been suggested by the current survey.

4   Examine the development of the town along Sailors' Walk/High Street; ascertain
  whether this was a later suburb or contemporary with the core of the medieval
  burgh.

5   Investigate the extent of the kirkyard of the parish church, Kirk Wynd; more
  generally, ascertain whether any remains of earlier structures survive in the
  vicinity of the church of St Bryce, including any traces of the thirteenth-century
  church.

6   Ascertain the nature of the medieval harbour and the seventeenth-century harbours,
  then known as the 'old' and 'new' harbours (as noted above, this should be
  undertaken in conjunction with further historical research in the burgh records).

areas for further archaeological research

1   The **raised beaches** along the Fife coast have attracted considerable interest and
  research amongst geographers, particularly in the 1960s and 1970s. See, for
  example, D E Smith, 'Late and Post Glacial Changes of Shoreline on the
  Northern Side of the Forth Valley and Estuary' (University of Edinburgh Ph D
  thesis, 1965). A more detailed study of the raised beaches at Kirkcaldy, and the
  relationship between the natural topography and the development of the
  settlement here, is perhaps an avenue for further research. This would not only
  help to explain the morphology of the burgh, but might also pinpoint areas
  where archaeological deposits are likely to have accumulated and been preserved,
  for example at the base of a natural slope. Eventually, with the accumulation of
  more archaeological, geological, topographical and other physical data, a model
  could be developed of the underlying natural topography and surviving
  archaeological deposits within the burgh.

2   The **maritime history and archaeology** of Kirkcaldy clearly warrant further
  investigation, as described above (*see* p 67).

Some streets of interest are outwith the central core of historic Kirkcaldy. They are, therefore, included in the following list, but are not accompanied by an *area reference*.

Abbotshall Road Abbot's Walk	Malcolm III gifted the shire of Kirkcaladunt (Kirkcaldy) to the church of Dunfermline. The abbot of Dunfermline built a hall in what is now Raith Estate.
Adam Smith Close	*Area 1* Adam Smith, the world-famous economist, was born in Kirkcaldy in 1723.
Boswell's Wynd	*Areas 4 and 5* Situated to the west of the West Port, it was named after Richard Boswell and first mentioned in 1608, when the High Street was to be paved up to Boswell's Wynd. The work was not carried out until 1617.
Broad Wynd	*Pathhead* A wynd was a narrow thoroughfare. This was wider than the norm.
Bute Wynd	*Area 2* An area originally known as Abbotswynd, which was later corrupted to Boots Wynd and then Bute Wynd.
Charlotte Street	*Area 2* George III (1738–1820) married Charlotte of Mecklenburg-Strelitz in 1761.
Coal Wynd	*Areas 5 and 6* Coal came from the Lina Pit at Johnny Marshall's Loan and was brought down through the town to the harbour via Coal Wynd.
Commercial Street	*Pathhead* Lying behind Mid Street and Nether Street, it was originally known as Back Street. When it became a centre for shops and offices, the name was changed to Commercial Street.
Cross Vennel	*Areas 1 and 4* First mentioned in 1598. The market cross stood nearby.
Dishington's Wynd	*Areas 4 and 5* Now called Oswald's Wynd. It marked the eastern boundary of property once owned by the important Oswald family.
Douglas Street	*Area 3* Named after George Douglas, merchant in the town. He was one of four men who feued land from William Beveridge of Whytehouse, Park Place.
Dunnikier Road/Way	*Area 6* Dunnikier was the name given to the Pathhead region.
Esplanade, The	*Areas 1 and 2* Running parallel to the coastline of Kirkcaldy, this street was known as Sands Road until 1923.

72

Fish Wynd	*Area 6* The local fishermen and women reputedly had their homes in this street.
Flesh Wynd	*Pathhead* Originally, near the shore at Ravenscraig, there were whale oil boiling sheds. Subsequently, until 1865, these sheds were used as slaughter houses.
Gas Wynd	*Area 2* Until 1981 this was the site of the gas tank.
George Burn Wynd	*Area 1* This wynd was originally called Balcanquhal Burn after George Balcanquhal.
Glasswork Street	*Area 2* Presumably glassworks stood in this area, but no evidence has been found.
Heggie's Wynd	*Linktown* Heggie was a linen manufacturer in Linktown.
Hendry's Wynd	*Area 2* Named after William Hendry, who had a spinning mill at West Bridge in 1828.
High Street	*Areas 1, 2, 3, 4, 5 and 6* So called because it is the main thoroughfare in the town.
Hill Vennel Hill Place Hill Street	*Areas 3 and 4* These streets were built on hilly terrain.
Hunter Street	*Areas 3 and 4* John Hunter (1831–1916) was a joiner by trade. He purchased St Brycedale House from Provost Swan and gifted it to Kirkcaldy as a hospital.
Kirk Wynd	*Area 4* Takes its name from the church in the street.
Links Street	*Linktown* This street lies in Linktown and was built on undulating, sandy ground near the sea-shore.
Louden's Wynd	*Area 2* First mentioned in 1609. John Louden owned one of the factories in Linktown. Until 1876 this wynd marked the boundary between Kirkcaldy Burgh and Linktown.
Malcolm's Wynd	*Area 6* Provost Malcolm was engaged in a firm of ship owners and builders. In 1825 he had six ships, the largest fleet owned by a Kirkcaldy man.

Mariners' Street	*Area 6* Sited near the harbour, frequented by sailors.
Methven Road	*Linktown* Named after David Methven, owner of the Links Pottery in the eighteenth and nineteenth centuries.
Mid Street	*Pathhead* Mid Street lies between Nether Street and Commercial Street.
Mill Street	*Linktown* Named after the mills located along this street.
Milton Road	*Area 3* Milton or Mylntoun was mentioned in 1539 when Thomas Scott of Pitgorno was ceded the lands of Abbotshall and Mylntoun.
Nether Street	*Pathhead* 'Nether' originally meant low or lower.
Nicol Street	*Area 3* Originally known as Newton, its name was changed to Nicol Street after Nicol, the linen manufacturer in the Links.
Oswald's Wynd	*Areas 4 and 5* First mentioned in 1791, after the Oswalds of Dunnikier. This was originally known as Dishington's Wynd. Sometime after 1820 the wynd was renamed Oswald's Wynd, after Sir John Oswald who bought the property where the Co-op was later sited, to be his town house—Dunnikier House being too far out to allow him to be eligible to be a town councillor.
Path, The	*Area 6* The path leading from the centre of the town to Pathhead and Dysart.
Prime Gilt Box Street	First mentioned in 1591. Named after the fund to support mariners and their families in need.
Ravenscraig Street	*Pathhead* Named after the castle.
Redburn Wynd	*Area 1* Originally known as Red Burn.
St Brycedale Avenue St Brycedale Road	Named after St Bryce.
St Mary's Place St Mary's Road	*Area 6* So named as standing near the site of a supposed priory.
Spout Wynd	First mentioned in 1617, when cattle and horses were prohibited from fouling the wynd.
School Wynd	*Area 2* Situated near a school.

74

Tolbooth Street	*Areas 1 and 2* Eighteenth-century street. The tolbooth stood at its head.
Townsend Crescent Townsend Place	*Areas 4 and 5* At one time it was the outer limit of the town.
Volunteers' Green	The area of town green where the militia trained.
Webster's Wynd	Located to the west of the cross, it was named after William Webster, and first mentioned in 1659.
Wemyssfield	In 1773, Dr Alex Wemyss owned land at the head of Whytescauseway. He objected to the land being used as a thoroughfare, so a stone dyke was placed round it.
West Wynd	*Pathhead* West Wynd is the most westerly wynd leading from Nairn Street to Nether Street in Pathhead.
White's Wynd	Named after Robert White, provost in 1657.
Whytehouse Avenue	*Area 3* Robert Whyte, or Quhite, was provost of Kirkcaldy in 1657.
Whytescauseway	*Area 3* A causeway is a pathway raised and paved with stone. Robert Whyte was provost of Kirkcaldy in 1657.

alderman	Chief burghal officer, sometimes *prepositus*, later provost.
almshouse	House for the support and lodging of the poor; sometimes a hospital.
artefact	Any portable object used, modified or made by humans (*eg* pottery, tools, weapons, jewellery, *etc*).
assemblage	Group of artefacts.
backlands	The area to the rear of the burgage plot behind the dwelling house on the frontage. Originally intended for growing produce and keeping animals; site of wells and midden heaps. Eventually housed working premises of craftsmen and poorer members of burgh society.
back yett	Small gate in fencing at end of toft, giving access to burgh common land and countryside.
bailie	Burgh officers who performed routine administration, often under an alderman or *prepositus*.
baxter	Baker.
booth	Small open-fronted stall, sometimes free-standing but often appended to the front of houses lining the street, where merchants and craftsmen sold their goods.
boundaries	*see* burgage plot
burgage plot	A division of land, often of regular size, having been measured out by liners, allocated to a burgess. Once built on, it contained the burgage house on the frontage (*see* frontage) and a backland (*see* backland). In time, with pressure for space, the plots were often subdivided—repletion. Plots were bounded by ditches, wattle fences or stone walls.
burgess	Person who enjoyed the privileges and responsibilities of the freedom of the burgh.
burgh ferme	Rental on burgh property.
buttis (bow buttis)	Ground set aside for archery practice.
close	*see* vennel
common ground	Revenues from the burgh courts, the fishings, multures, market tolls, rentals, *etc*.
cordiner	Leather worker.
craft	Trade.
documentary sources	Written evidence, primary sources being the original documents.
drift	A geological term which describes anything transported and

76

deposited by wind, water or ice; for example, boulder clay, sands and gravels.

environmental remains
Usually defines non-artefactual evidence from a site, for example, bones, seeds, pollen, parasite eggs.

excavation
Principal method of data acquisition in archaeology, including the systematic uncovering of archaeological remains through the removal of soil and other material covering them and accompanying them.

façade
Finished face of a building.

feu-ferme
Payment of burghal dues to the burgh superior by a pre-agreed annual sum.

fill
Term used in bore hole surveys to describe man-made or artificial deposits, and could include those relating to the medieval period or earlier.

frontage
Front part of burgage plot nearest the street, on which the dwelling was usually built.

gap site
Burgage plot not built up or 'biggit'; in a modern context, undeveloped space between two buildings.

guild
Organisation or fraternity for mutual support, whether economic, religious or social.

hammerman
Metal worker and associated craftsman.

heid-dyke
Small, contiguous fencing at tail-end of toft, often containing small back yett, or gate, giving access to burgh common land and countryside.

hinterland
Rural area around a burgh, to which the burgh looked for economic and agricultural support; hinterland likewise dependent on burgh market.

humic soil
Soil with a high organic content.

indweller
Unprivileged, non-burgess dweller in a town.

liner
Burgh officer with responsibility to measure burgage plots and supervise building matters.

market repletion
The use of an open market area for building when space within the town became limited.

merk
13s 4d, two-thirds of £ Scots.

midden
Accumulation of debris and domestic waste products resulting from human use.

multure
Payment for use of town mills.

natural	The level of subsoil undisturbed by human activity.	77
pend	Narrow close or walkway between buildings.	
port	Gate to town; shut at night and in times of plague and external danger; usually a simple wooden structure; occasionally a more elaborate stone feature.	
prehistory	Period of human history before the advent of writing.	
repletion	*see* burgage plot	
regality burgh	Burgh which had superior other than the crown.	
rig	*see* burgage plot	
scarping	Removal of earth, often to provide level ground prior to building.	
sherd	Fragment of pottery.	
slag	Material residue of smelting process from metal-working.	
soffit	Ornamented underside of a stair, archway, etc.	
stratification	Laying down or depositing of strata or layers (also called deposits) one above the other; a succession of layers should provide a relative chronological sequence, with the earliest at the bottom and the latest at the top.	
stratigraphy	Study of stratification.	
tectonic movements	Displacements in the earth's crust.	
toft	*see* burgage plot	
tolbooth	The most important secular building; meeting place of burgh council; collection post for market tolls; often housed town gaol.	
toll	Payment for use of burgh market.	
townhouse	Principal modern civic building.	
tron	Public weigh-beam.	
urban nucleus	Original site(s) from which town developed.	
vennel	Alley; narrow lane.	
Wattle wattle and daub post and wattle	Method of constructing wooden fence or wall in which pliable branches (wattle) are woven in between upright posts; as reinforcement or insulation layers of clay, mud and animal dung (daub) were applied to the wattle surface; wattle was also used to line pits, wells, drains and other constructions such as ovens.	
£	£ Scots, which by 1603 was valued at one-twelfth of £ sterling.	

Kirkcaldy District Archive
Burgh Court Books 1.6.1–8 (1568–1635).
Council Minutes 1.1.2 (1663–80).
Presbytery Records (Seventeenth Century).
Trades Council Books 1.9.1–5 (Seventeenth Century).

Scottish Record Office
E69/10/2 Hearth Tax Records.

printed primary sources

Accounts of the Lord High Treasurer of Scotland, 13 vols, edd T Dickson *et al* (Edinburgh, 1877–).
Accounts of the Masters of Works for Building and Repairing Royal Palaces and Castles, 2 vols, edd H
    M Paton *et al* (Edinburgh, 1957–82).
The Acts of the Parliaments of Scotland, 12 vols, edd T Thomson & C Innes (Edinburgh,
    1814–1875).
Anderson, A O (ed), *Early Sources of Scottish History, AD 500 to 1286*, 2 vols (Stamford,
    1990).
Bain, J (ed), *Calendar of Documents Relating to Scotland*, 4 vols (Edinburgh, 1881–8).
Bain, J (ed), *The Hamilton Papers: Letters and Papers Illustrating the Political Relations of England
    and Scotland in the Sixteenth Century*, 2 vols (Edinburgh, 1892).
Ballard, A & Tait, J (edd), *British Borough Charters, 1216–1307* (Cambridge, 1923).
Beveridge, E (ed), *The Burgh Records of Dunfermline* (Edinburgh, 1917).
Calendar of the Laing Charters, AD 854–1837, ed J Anderson (Edinburgh, 1899).
Calendar of State Papers, Domestic (London, 1858–).
Defoe, D, *A Tour Through the Whole Island of Great Britain*, edd P Furbank & W R Owens
    (London, 1991; orig pub 1724).
The Exchequer Rolls of Scotland, 23 vols, edd J Stuart *et al* (Edinburgh, 1878–1908).
Extracts from the Records of the Burgh of Edinburgh, 1655 to 1665, ed M Wood (Edinburgh,
    1940).
Extracts from the Records of the Burgh of Glasgow, ix, 1796–1808, ed J Renwick (Glasgow,
    1914).
Extracts from the Records of The Royal Burgh of Stirling, 1667–1752 (Glasgow, Stirlingshire and
    Sons of the Rock Society, 1899).
Fraser, W, *The Melvilles, Earls of Melville and the Leslies, Earls of Leven*, vol iii (Edinburgh,
    1890).
Fraser, W, *Memorials of the Family of Wemyss of Wemyss*, vol ii (Edinburgh, 1888).
Hamilton, G, *The House of Hamilton*, vol ii (Edinburgh, 1933).
Heron, R, *Scotland Delineated* (Edinburgh, 1975; orig pub 1799).
Hume Brown, P (ed), *Early Travellers in Scotland* (Edinburgh, 1891).
Hume Brown, P (ed), *Scotland before 1700 from Contemporary Documents* (Edinburgh, 1893).
Leges Burgorum, in *Ancient Laws and Customs of the Burghs of Scotland, 1124–1424*, ed C Innes
    (Scottish Burgh Records Society, 1868).
MacBean, L (ed), *The Kirkcaldy Burgh Records* (Kirkcaldy, 1908).
Mackie, J D (ed), *The Calendar of State Papers relating to Scotland and Mary Queen of Scots*, vol
    xiii, part ii (Edinburgh, 1969).
Pococke, R, *Tours in Scotland 1747, 1750, 1760*, ed D W Kemp (SHS, 1887).
*The Presbyterie Booke of Kirkcaldie, Being the Record of the Proceedings of that Presbytery from the
    Fifteenth Day of April 1630 to the Fourteenth day of September 1653*, ed W Stevenson
    (Kirkcaldy, 1900).
The Records of the Convention of Royal Burghs of Scotland, 7 vols, ed J D Marwick (Edinburgh,
    1866–1918).

Regesta Regum Scotorum:

> vol i *The Acts of Malcolm IV, King of Scots, 1153–1165*, ed G W S Barrow (Edinburgh, 1960).

> vol ii *The Acts of William I, King of Scots, 1165–1214*, ed G W S Barrow with W W Scott (Edinburgh, 1971).

> vol v *The Acts of Robert I, King of Scots, 1306–1329*, ed A A M Duncan (Edinburgh, 1988).

> vol vi *The Acts of David II, King of Scots, 1329–1371*, ed B Webster (Edinburgh, 1982).

'Register containing the state and condition of every burgh within the kingdom of Scotland in the year 1692', in *Scottish Burgh Records Society Miscellany* (1881).

The Register of the Great Seal of Scotland, 11 vols, edd J M Thomson *et al* (Edinburgh, 1882–1914).

The Register of the Privy Council of Scotland, edd J H Burton *et al:* first series, 14 vols (Edinburgh, 1877–98), second series, 8 vols (Edinburgh, 1899–1908), third series, 16 vols (Edinburgh, 1908–).

The Register of the Privy Seal of Scotland (Registrum Secreti Sigilli Regum Scotorum), 8 vols, edd M Livingston *et al* (Edinburgh, 1908–).

Registrum de Dunfermelyn, ed C Innes (Bannatyne Club, 1842).

Report on the Burgh of Kirkcaldy, Fifeshire, to Accompany the Reform Act of 1832 (Historical Discovery, Crewe).

Selections from the Minutes of the Synod of Fife, 1611–1687, ed G R Kinloch (Abbotsford Club, 1837).

Statute Gilde in *Ancient Laws and Customs of the Burghs of Scotland, 1124–1424*, ed C Innes (Scottish Burgh Records Society, 1868).

Stuart, J (ed), *Records of the Monastery of Kinloss* (Society of Antiquaries of Scotland, 1872).

The Statistical Account of Scotland 1791–9, vol x, *Fife*, ed J Sinclair. New edition, edd D J Withrington & I R Grant, (Wakefield, 1978). (The Kirkcaldy entry is at pp 505–54, written by the Rev. Thomas Fleming in 1792.)

The New Statistical Account of Scotland, vol ix, *Fife and Kinross* (Edinburgh, 1845) (at pp 740–70, written by Rev J Alexander).

Torrie, E P Dennison (ed), *The Gild Court Book of Dunfermline, 1433–1597* (Scottish Record Society, 1986).

Webster, J M & Duncan, A A M (edd), *The Regality of Dunfermline Court Book* (Dunfermline, 1953).

secondary sources

Bateson, M, *Borough Customs*, 2 vols (Selden Society, 1904).

Breeze, D J, *The Northern Frontiers of Roman Britain* (London, 1982).

Brown, C J & Shipley, B M, *Soil Survey of Scotland: South-East Scotland. 1:2500 000 Sheet 7. Soil and Land Capability for Agriculture* (The Macaulay Institute for Soil Research, Aberdeen, 1982).

Caldwell, D (ed), *Scottish Weapons and Fortifications, 1100–1800* (Edinburgh, 1981).

Cameron, I B & Stephenson, D, *The Midland Valley of Scotland* (3rd edn, British Regional Geology, Natural Environment Research Council, London, 1985).

Campbell, J, Richardson, A T, MacGregor, G, Deas, G & MacBean, L, *Kirkcaldy Burgh and Schyre: Landmarks of Local History* (Kirkcaldy, 1924).

Cruden, S, *The Scottish Castle* (3rd edn, Edinburgh, 1981).

Darvill, T, *Prehistoric Britain* (London, 1987).

Discovery and Excavation in Scotland (Edinburgh, 1977, 1980, 1987, 1990, 1992 and 1993).

Dow, J, '*Skotter* in sixteenth-century Scania', *Scottish Historical Review*, xliv (1965).

Dow, J, 'Scottish trade with Sweden', *Scottish Historical Review*, xlviii (1969).

Duckham, B F, *A History of the Scottish Coal Industry*, vol i (Newton Abbot, 1970).   81

Eunson, E, *Bygone Fife* (Glasgow, 1910).

Farnie, H, *The Handy Book of the Fife Coast* (n d).

Fife's Early Archaeological Heritage (Fife Regional Council, 1989).

Groome, F H, *Ordnance Gazetteer of Scotland: A Survey of Scottish Topography*, 6 vols (Edinburgh, 1886).

Irvine, J, *Kirkcaldy Old Parish Church, 1244–1944* (Kirkcaldy, 1994).

Kirkcaldy Area Local Plan (Kirkcaldy District Council, 1993).

Kirkcaldy Origin of Street Names (Kirkcaldy Civic Society, 1975).

Livingstone, P K, *A History of Kirkcaldy* (Kirkcaldy, 1955).

Lockhart, J Y, *Kirkcaldy Burgh and Harbour: An Historical Outline* (Kirkcaldy, 1940).

Lynch, M, 'Urbanisation and urban networks in seventeenth-century Scotland: some further thoughts', *Scottish Economic and Social History*, xii (1992).

Lynch, M, 'Continuity and change in urban society, 1500–1700', in R A Houston & I D Whyte (edd), *Scottish Society, 1500–1800* (Cambridge, 1989).

Lythe, S G E, *The Economy of Scotland in its European Setting, 1550–1625* (Edinburgh, 1960).

Mair, C, *Mercat Cross and Tolbooth* (Edinburgh, 1988).

Maxwell, G S , *The Romans in Scotland* (Edinburgh, 1989).

Megaw, J V S & Simpson, D D A, *Introduction to British Prehistory* (Leicester, 1979).

Pearson, J M, *Around Kirkcaldy* (Kirkcaldy, 1993).

Price, R J, *Scotland's Environment During the Last 30,000 Years* (Edinburgh, 1983).

Pride, G L, *The Kingdom of Fife: An Illustrated Architectural Guide* (Edinburgh, 1990).

Pryde, G S, *The Burghs of Scotland: A Critical List* (Oxford, 1965).

Robertson, A S, 'Roman coins found in Scotland', *PSAS*, xcvi (1960–1).

Robertson, A S, 'Roman coins found in Scotland', *PSAS*, ciii (1970–1).

Robertson, A S, 'Roman coins found in Scotland', *PSAS*, cxiii (1983).

Royal Commission on the Ancient and Historical Monuments of Scotland, *Eleventh Report with Inventory of Monuments and Constructions in the Counties of Fife, Kinross, and Clackmannan* (Edinburgh, 1933)

Scrimgeour, R, Nos *339–343 High Street, Kirkcaldy. Record and Analysis for the Scottish Historic Buildings Trust* (Kirkcaldy, 1993).

Simpson, W D, *Ravenscraig Castle* (Aberdeen University Studies, n d), no 115.

Simpson, W D, *Ravenscraig Castle* (Transactions of the Glasgow Archaeological Society, New Series, viii).

Sissons, J B, *The Geomorphology of the British Isles: Scotland* (London, 1976).

Smith, D E, 'Late and Post Glacial Changes of Shoreline on the Northern Side of the Forth Valley and Estuary' (University of Edinburgh PhD thesis, 1965).

Smout, T C, *Scottish Trade on the Eve of Union, 1660–1707* (Edinburgh, 1963).

Stell, G, 'Late medieval defences in Scotland', in D H Caldwell (ed), *Scottish Weapons and Fortifications, 1100–1800* (Edinburgh, 1981).

Stevenson, W, *The Presbyterie Booke of Kirkcaldie* (Kirkcaldy, 1990).

Torrie, E P Dennison, 'The Gild of Dunfermline in the Fifteenth Century' (Unpublished University of Edinburgh PhD thesis, 1984).

'Webster's Analysis of Population', in *Scottish Population Statistics* (SHS, 1952).

Whatley, C A, *The Scottish Salt Industry, 1570–1850* (Aberdeen, 1987).

Whyte, I D, 'Urbanization in early-modern Scotland: a preliminary analysis', *Scottish Economic and Social History*, ix (1989).

unpublished archaeological reports

Trial Excavations at 15 The Esplanade, Kirkcaldy (SUAT, 1994).

A Watching Brief at 113 High Street, Kirkcaldy (SUAT, 1993).

Trial Excavations at Sea-View House, Oswald's Wynd, Kirkcaldy (SUAT, 1994).

cartographic sources

'A Map of Central Scotland from the River Tummel to Glasgow, and from Loch Long to Broughty Ferry', by Robert Gordon of Straloch, *c* 1630.

'Fife', by James Gordon, 1642.

'Fifae Vicecomitatus', in J Blaeu, *Atlas Novus* (Amsterdam, 1654).

'Fifae Pars Occidentalis', in J Blaeu, *Atlas Novus* (Amsterdam, 1654).

'Fifeshire', by John Ainslie, 1775.

17:5 and 18:1 of General Roy's maps, 1747–55.

'Plan of the Royal Burgh of Kirkcaldy', by Richard Moore, 1809.

'Plan of the Town of Kirkcaldy', by John Wood, 1824.

'Plan of Kirkcaldy', from *Accounts and Papers relating to Parliamentary Representation, 1831–32*.

'The Town of Kirkcaldy', Ordnance Survey Map, 1856.

Ordnance Survey 1:10,000, 1983.

Ordnance Survey 1:2,500.

Ordnance Survey, *Map of Roman Britain* (Southampton, 1978).

84